THE FACEBO

THE FACEBOOK MANAGER

The Psychology and Practice of Web-based Social Networking

Bridget Grenville-Cleave
&
Jonathan Passmore

First published in 2009 by Management Books 2000 Ltd
Forge House, Limes Road
Kemble, Cirencester
Gloucestershire, GL7 6AD, UK
Tel: 0044 (0) 1285 771441
Fax: 0044 (0) 1285 771055
Email: info@mb2000.com
Web: www.mb2000.com

British Library Cataloguing in Publication Data is available

ISBN 9781852526252

About the authors

Bridget Grenville-Cleave

Bridget Grenville-Cleave is a management consultant, trainer and facilitator with a passion for personal and organisational change. She lectures in Applied Positive Psychology at the University of East London, UK, where she recently gained an MSc. Bridget has written her own Positive Psychology blog since 2006, and contributes to the online journal, Positive Psychology News Daily. Her first book, the Happiness Equation: a scientific look at the top one hundred factors that can add to or subtract from your happiness, was published in 2008. She has an MBA from the Open University Business School. Bridget can be contacted at: bridget@workmad.co.uk, via LinkedIn, Facebook or Twitter (bridgetgc).

Dr Jonathan Passmore

Jonathan Passmore is a chartered occupational psychologist, an associate fellow of the British Psychology Society, a fellow of the Chartered Institute of Personnel and Development and has five degrees. He has wide business experience having worked for PricewaterhouseCoopers, IBM and OPM, and as a chief executive and company chairman in the sports and leisure sector. He is based at the University of East London, UK and is Director for the Coaching Psychology programmes. He has written widely in magazines, peer reviewed journals and is the author / editor of 12 books including titles on organisational change and coaching. He can be contacted at: jonathancpassmore@yahoo.co.uk.

Acknowledgements

Writing this book has required considerable help, support and encouragement from a host of others and we would like to say thank you in particular to our partners Katharine and Neil, to Stefan Cantore for his contributions at the start of this process and in identifying the need for such a book, to Nick Dale-Harris from MB2000 for his help in steering the book to publication, and to Kathryn Britton, Benjamin Ellis, Willy Franzen, David Jones, Mike Morrison and Yang-May Ooi for their contributions, suggestions and encouragement.

Contents

Foreword

It was an accident. I recently sent several hundred people a 'smiley sun' when all I intended to do was cheer up my friend Jane! It just goes to show that we need to understand how to properly use social networking sites.

It could have been much worse. There are plenty of examples in this practical book that demonstrate what can happen when you don't understand what you are doing. An inappropriate picture, a rude comment about your boss and even telling the world that you are going on holiday can lead to unforeseen consequences. Dismissal from your job and your house being burgled are possible outcomes. Apparently some smart thieves are now using social networking to identify who of us may have left our houses empty for a couple of weeks!

What makes this book a great read is the way the authors dwell on the positive aspects of social networking whilst highlighting potential pitfalls we need to be aware of. They set out a strong case for why individuals and organisations should see Facebook and sites like it as a time and cost effective means to achieving a specific goal. If you want a new job or your company wants to boost morale by creating a stronger team spirit then the answer may be found in creating powerful networks that really connect people.

For someone like me who may be a little uncertain about how exactly to use social networking in a business context then this book is a real gift. The authors encourage us to think through why we may want to do it in the first place and then, in simple language, help us navigate the practicalities of social networking.

My passion at work is to help people have powerful heart to heart conversations. *The Facebook Manager* opens our minds to the huge potential of such conversations held across the globe. They are the key to stimulating change at a rate we could never have conceived of a generation ago. Read this book and get on and network!

Stefan Cantore
Office for Public Management, London

1

The Manager as Networker

'It's not what you know, it's who you know'

Never has this adage been more important than today. When we first started working, we didn't take much notice of it, being naive 20-somethings, fresh out of university anxiously clutching our degree certificates and eager to land a job which acknowledged the years we'd spent getting our qualifications and which, of course, paid well, had good prospects and was interesting too. We didn't really believe that who you know could possibly be more important than our enthusiasm, our willingness to learn, and our obvious (to us!) talents.

And here we are, some two decades later, thinking back to those days and wondering what we would have done differently if we'd taken more notice of that maxim.

How the world of work is changing

It's curious to note that, in the intervening twenty years, much has changed about the world of work, and yet some things have not. A huge number of organisations are now global, industrialised and computerised. The growth and spread of the internet has created a more level playing field for business (or at any rate, has enabled thousands of small niche businesses to spring up). Employment for many in the West is more flexible, more competitive, more casual (in dress) more target driven, faster and, dare we say it, much more complex. Even the professions themselves, whether health, education or engineering, have changed significantly, largely due to the impact of information and communications technology (ICT). We're not necessarily talking technical skills here either, although they play a part. You can't get far in many jobs these days without a PC and access to the internet. Ironically, the rise of ICT in business has forced some to become more skilled at dealing with people, as we shall see in the example given below.

Accountants in the limelight

Take the accounting profession as an example. ICT has transformed it almost beyond recognition. When I was studying for my professional qualifications in the early 1990s, the biggest change expected as a result of ICT was the so-called 'paperless office' (in fact the reverse seems to have happened, but that's another story). Few foresaw the huge change that would occur in the day-to-day functions of the finance department and, as a result, to the accountant's role, and subsequently to the type of personality best suited to that role.

Nowadays, there aren't many accountants (particularly in the corporate environment) who can sit quietly ticking boxes or checking lists of figures all day even if that's what they wanted to do, since most of this type of detailed work is done by software programmes. In management-speak the finance function now acts as a business partner, which has had a serious knock-on impact on the accountant's role. Gone are the days when accountants were quiet, introvert backroom boys (or girls) who had little to do with the real business from one month to the next. Now they're expected to be cool, credible and confident enough to sit at the same boardroom table as the directors of sales, marketing and operations.

Some might say that the only thing that hasn't really changed is the accountant's love of grey!

So as a result, the accountant in 2009 is a very different animal to the accountant in 1989. They need to be as adept at handling people as they are at dealing with numbers. They need to be able to stand up and present financial budgets, forecasts and plans in a concise, coherent and compelling style to large groups of senior managers and executives. And they need to be able to present themselves as savvy, poised and professional people, who can work with the top team as easily as they can with the office 5-a-side team. So accountants in business nowadays must demonstrate a very different skill-set. Of course it almost goes without saying that they have to have all the technical financial knowledge and ability, but they also need a whole range of personal and interpersonal skills if they're going to be successful and make their way to the top of their organisation or profession. And professional accounting qualifications have had to change to reflect the transformation in the accountant's business role; they now include subjects like techniques for improving personal effectiveness at work, leadership, management and supervision, and motivating individuals and teams.

If you look at the development of any profession over the past couple of decades, you can probably identify similar remarkable transformations.

And yet despite seismic changes in the business world, there are some important things about working in organisations that we believe haven't altered all that much. We still passionately believe that it's who you know not what you know that is likely to make the biggest difference to your effectiveness and success at work, so this book will be useful both to those established managers who want to learn how to make the most of their connections at work, and those who are just starting out in the employment world. We would even go so far as to say that effective networking, and associated social skills have never been more important than they are today. Building and maintaining strong connections with friends, colleagues and associates are as important as making the right career choice; everyone who is serious about their success in the workplace needs to appreciate this.

Growth of the Internet, ICT and Social Networks

It's helpful here to wind back a few years and put the internet, ICT and the new social networks into context. If you're from the Y Generation (born in or after 1980) you might find it hard to believe that back in the 1980s PCs were not a common feature, and mobile phones were barely that – the first commercial mobile, invented by Motorola, was about the size of a brick and cost some $4000 (in 1983 prices). One of us had a job in 1986 which required us to carry the organisation's only mobile phone at weekends and deal with emergencies, and the response from people when it rang on a train is very different to today. Many businesses operated their financial systems on large mainframe computers, housed in specially air-conditioned rooms and accessed using stand-alone terminals. Financial transactions were batch processed, often overnight so as not to interrupt the day's work, with error or exception reports being produced the following morning. PCs as we know them today did not come into widespread use in business until the early to mid 1990s. Many of the smaller businesses still used paper. 'Cutting and pasting' was literally that, using scissors and glue! One of our colleagues recalls creating a presentation like this; Powerpoint had not yet been invented. There was email, of a sort – it was originally restricted to in-house usage, so if you wanted to contact third parties outside the business you still had to phone or write a letter. And before Windows became the generic business software operating system, PCs were operated using the text-based MS-DOS (Microsoft Disk Operating System), whereby the computer was given instructions by manually entering text into the command line interface. In those days you had to understand computer language. Today of course, graphical user interfaces like Windows translate our commands for us. And as for the internet, well although it seems to have been with us forever, it only appeared in mainstream business use from the late 1990s. Around 1997, one of us remembers presenting a paper as a director to our board proposing to create a web page for the business and the idea being rejected as a waste of money. The company now has dozens of pages of online text plus forms and information sheets to download as pdf documents. Nowadays, few business people could imagine working without the internet let alone email and their PC, Blackberry or mobile phone.

The Internet going global?

The advancement of ICT in business has been credited with the increased productivity seen in the Western world in the past decade or so. In the UK for example, extra productivity gains are associated with more widespread use of computers. Government statistics[1] show that manufacturing companies achieve an extra 2.2% productivity for each additional 10% of employees using computers. In newer firms, this extra productivity effect rises to 4.4%. The effect associated with internet use is greater, where companies achieve an extra 2.9%. Again, for newer firms the effect is larger. According to the International Telecommunications Union[2], approximately 24% (1.6bn) of the world's population is now online, although you can't talk about global internet statistics these days without mentioning the digital divide: in North America, 74% of the population use the internet, whereas Europe stands at about 48%, Australasia at 60% and Africa a mere 5%. It's not just the percentages that matter, however, the absolute figures are important here. The population of Asia makes up more than half the world, so even at only 18% internet usage, the number of users there already exceeds that in North America. And the final number of Asian internet users (or netizens as they are sometimes called) will significantly outweigh those in the West. This explains why

[1] http://www.statistics.gov.uk/cci/nugget.asp?id=1240
[2] http://www.itu.int/ITU-D/ict/statistics/ict/index.html

some experts predict that Chinese will overtake English as the first language of the internet. In July 2009, Baidu.com[3], the Chinese language search engine, and QQ.com[4], the Chinese instant messaging (IM) and social networking website, were rated 9th and 14th largest websites (as measured by a combination of page views and visitors) in the world[5]. The predicted increase in Asian internet users is likely to change the webscape dramatically, whether or not Western organisations are successful in translating their websites into the many Asian languages[6]. And in October 2009, the regulator Icann announced that it had approved plans to allow the use of Arabic, Chinese and other non-Latin scripts in internet addresses, a move described as the biggest shake-up since the internet was created 40 years ago.[7]

The rise of Social Networking sites[8]

And what about social networking sites like Facebook, MySpace and Bebo, business networking sites like LinkedIn, Ecademy and Xing, and profession-specific networks like Lawlink[9], Land Surveyors United[10], Mendeley[11] and DoctorsHangout[12], are they really as popular as media reports and technology gurus would have us

[3] http://www.baidu.com

[4] http://www.qq.com

[5] http://www.alexa.com/topsites

[6] http://www.nytimes.com/2008/12/31/technology/internet/31hindi.html?pagewanted=1&_r=1&sq=Writing%20the%20Web%C3%83%C2%A2%C3%A2%E2%80%9A%C2%AC%C3%A2%E2%80%9E%C2%A2s%20Future%20in%20Numerous%20Languages&st=Search&scp=2

[7] http://news.bbc.co.uk/1/hi/technology/8333194.stm

[8] It's worth pointing out that academics often refer to Social Network Sites, rather than Social Networking Sites since research suggests that they are not used primarily for finding new friends or contacts, but for keeping in touch with existing ones. In this book, we don't make that distinction.

[9] http://www.lawlink.com/

[10] http://landsurveyorsunited.ning.com/

[11] http://www.mendeley.com/

[12] http://www.doctorshangout.com/

believe? US market research provider comscore.com[13] states global usage figures for key social networking sites as follows:

	Total Unique Visitors in millions		
	June 2007	*June 2008*	*% Change*
Total internet audience	778	861	11
Total social network audience	464	580	25
Facebook	52	132	153
MySpace	114	117	3
Bebo	18	24	32

It turns out that the exact number of global users is uncertain: according to *Computer Weekly*[14] in November 2008, Facebook had over 120 million users worldwide (of which 18.4 million were in the UK) and by end of January 2009, its own statistics[15] claimed over 150m members. Yet in November 2008, comscore reported that Facebook's membership had already reached 200m. Further contradictory information about membership numbers has been issued by one Facebook insider[16]. Even if these figures are somewhere in the right ballpark, we actually don't know if these millions of people are active, regular users of the site, or just people who log on once, have a look and log off, never to be seen again. The same uncertainty surrounds the Myspace and other social networking site statistics. The only thing we can say for certain is that usage is huge, and growing.

[13] www.comscore.com
[14] http://www.computerweekly.com/Articles/2009/01/16/234276/facebook-what-future-for-social-networks.htm
[15] http://www.facebook.com/press/info.php?statistics
[16] http://twitter.com/davemorin/statuses/898779449

What is the take up of social networking sites worldwide?

According to the web information company, Alexa.com[17], social networking sites are amongst the top websites in the world, having the most internet visitors and page views, with memberships running into millions, and users spending an increasing amount of time there.

Alexa.com global rank	Website	Reach (% global internet users who visit this site / 3 month avg)	Avg time spent (mins/day)
4	Facebook	18.9%	26.2
11	MySpace	4.7%	19.4
14	Qzone/QQ (IM & social networking combined – China)	3.4%	9.9
25	Twitter	2.3%	8.4
29	V Kontakte (Russia)	1.4%	37.6
35	Hi5 (Mexico)	1.6%	22.4
89	LinkedIn	0.7%	6.5
324	Xing	0.2%	7.0

But even though Facebook and MySpace dominate in the West, it would be a mistake to assume that they are the most popular social networking sites in all countries. There is evidence[18] that

[17] http://wwww.alexa.com
[18] http://www.techcrunch.com/2009/06/07/a-map-of-social-network- dominance/

other sites are preferred in other parts of the world, for example: QQ in China, Orkut in India, Mixi in Japan and Cyworld in Korea.

If you're one of the Y Generation the chances are that you will already be a member of, and regular visitor to, at least one of these sites, perhaps several. If you're a member of the X Generation (born between 1960 and 1980) or a Baby Boomer (born before 1960) you might have dismissed using social networks as something that your children or young people do, not something that you even need to think about (other than the much reported and, it appears, vastly overstated concerns about grooming). So in a nutshell we outline what social networks are and aren't and why you should take social networking seriously.

How organisations have responded to the growth of Social Network sites

Whatever the global usage of social networking, we know that uptake in the workplace has been such that many organisations, both in the private and public sectors, are becoming increasingly concerned about how such sites are used by employees. There have been plenty of media stories surfacing in the past two to three years about organisations responding to the use of social networking sites at work by restricting them or banning them outright. The reasons given include:

- **Time wasting.** Frequently employers are concerned about the amount of time that their staff can spend on Facebook, MySpace and sites like them when they should be working. A study conducted by employment law firm, Peninsula, in 2007 suggested that the use of social networking sites at work was losing employers 233 million hours every month, the equivalent of £130m per day[19].
- Various social networking site applications take up **bandwidth** that is needed to operate company processes efficiently.

[19] http://news.bbc.co.uk/1/hi/technology/6989100.stm

- Giving away **sensitive information**. Employers are anxious that staff may be using social networking sites to discuss confidential work issues, and that the comments they post may be read by non-employees, consumers or even competitors.
- **Reputation management.** Careless or indiscrete postings on the part of corporate users might damage the company's reputation (see the Argos example below).
- **Security issues.** According to some technical experts, there is also a risk that computer viruses might be spread through using social network sites.

About Face

Birmingham City Council[20]

In January 2009, the *Birmingham Mail* reported that the City Council had banned the use of Facebook at work between the hours of 10am and noon and 2-4pm after it was found that staff were wasting hundreds of working hours a month on the site. Social networking sites weren't the only sites being frequently used by council workers (others being BBC, Sky Sports, Heart FM, Wikimedia and eBay), but the report doesn't clarify whether the Council has also banned access to these too.

Metropolitan Police Force

In July 2008, the *Daily Telegraph*[21] reported that the Metropolitan Police disciplined 18 of its officers for using

[20] http://www.birminghammail.net/news/top-stories/2009/01/20/facebook-ban-for-birmingham-city-council-workers-97319-22732433/
[21] http://www.telegraph.co.uk/news/uknews/2180276/Police-disciplined-for-Facebook-crash-

Facebook to boast about car crashes. The officers concerned had all joined a Facebook group called 'Look I've had a Polcol'. (Polcol is apparently slang for police collision.) According to the newspaper, the group also contained stories about collisions with pedestrians.

Northampton General Hospital

In October 2008, it was reported that Northampton General Hospital blocked access to all social networking sites after one of its night duty nurses posted a topless photo of herself on her Facebook page[22]. The nurse in question was disciplined.

In addition, media reports state that other well-known companies (such as Lloyds TSB, Credit Suisse, Goldman Sachs, Citigroup and British Gas) have either banned access to social networking sites altogether or have warned that using them during office hours is a dismissal offence.

Critics of corporate Facebook bans, however, suggest that companies are being over-zealous and short-sighted, and that preventing staff from accessing social networks at work will do more harm to employee relations than good. After all, an outright veto suggests that employees can't be trusted to do their jobs properly or to do the right thing at the right time, and that the organisation hasn't got the nous to deal appropriately with the few who do misuse their work time. There are some, such as California-based Serena[23], a global software company, which gives employees a free hour on Fridays to update their Facebook profiles – it's called a Facebook Friday. In response to concerns about employees using Facebook to post confidential information about the company, Serena's CEO, Jeremy Burton said 'If we have any devious

boasts.html

[22] http://www.telegraph.co.uk/technology/3358681/Facebook-ban-for-nurses-after-online-flashing.html

[23] http://www.serena.com

employees there are plenty of other ways they could get information out without Facebook... I think employees are generally honest, and if you treat them like adults, they'll take responsibility for what they do.'[24]

From a psychological perspective, it's not simply that putting social networking out of bounds is likely to increase its attractiveness, or that today's employees expect not to be told what to do and how to behave from one moment to the next. It's also to do with technology blurring the boundaries between personal and work lives which has been accelerating ever since email and mobile phones took off. If social networking is part of your personal life, it is also part of your work life. Employers who persist in trying to keep the two separate are behaving like King Canute.

More important than this, however, is the emerging research[25] which suggests that the social networking phenomenon, enabled by technology, is significantly changing the balance of power within society and organisations, and that those with so-called 'network capital' will be the real winners. You can no longer tell who wields the most influence in a company by looking at the top couple of lines of a company's organisation chart (organigram). According to Demos, what social networks and dynamics have started to do is to create new centres of power and influence at different points in the organisation, which means that they can be as important as, and often are more important than, the formal organisational hierarchy and structure in determining how information flows around the organisation, what work gets done, how and by whom. This, of course, means that social networks are forces for change, which the bosses and managers of many companies and other organisations find threatening. We suggest that those who prefer to fight against such change are doing so at considerable risk to their future success.

---

[24] http://www.internetnews.com/bus-news/article.php/3710336
http://www.fastforwardblog.com/2007/11/08/it-is-time-for-facebook-fridays-a-idea-that-should-spread/

[25] Bradwell, P & Reeves, R. (2008). Network citizens: power and responsibility at work. London. Demos

Company policy – for and against

In the UK, the Chartered Institute of Personnel and Development (which has its own 'corporate' Facebook site as well as numerous CIPD spin-off sites) advises organisations to produce a 'Facebook Policy', setting out the limits on the use of social networking sites at work. If access is allowed, they advise that the policy should clearly state that confidential matters should not be discussed and that any defamatory statements about the organisation will be treated as a disciplinary offence. That way, everyone knows where they stand. But should employers monitor their employees' use of social networking sites, whether in work or outside?

In a survey of social networking and reputational risk in the workplace, consulting firm Deloitte LLP found that 60% of the executives surveyed said they had the 'right to know' how employees portray themselves and their organisations online, whereas 53% of the employee respondents said that 'social networking pages are none of an employer's business', and nearly a third claimed that they never consider what the boss, their colleagues or clients would think before posting materials online. It is difficult to see how to reconcile such clearly divided opinion, especially since 49% of employees also claim that a company policy would not change how they behave online anyway.[26]

As we have suggested above, restricting access to new technologies is akin to shutting the stable door after the horse has bolted. Companies which adopt a head in the sand approach, ignoring the benefits of Web 2.0 technologies are missing a trick. Forward-thinking organisations such as Deloittes and IBM[27] use networking sites and internet forums in a way which enables communication, collaboration and innovation, and which ultimately increases business productivity.

[26] Deloitte LLP (April 2009). Social networking and reputational risk in the workplace. http://www.deloitte.com/dtt/cda/doc/content/us_2009_ethics_workplace_survey_150509.pdf

[27] http://computerworld.com/s/article/322857/The_new_employee_connection_Social_networking_behind_the_firewall

The arguments for and against banning Facebook raise the increasingly important question about public versus private information. Is searching Google or Facebook for the profile of a prospective employee an invasion of privacy? Some people would say yes. On the one hand it could be argued that, regardless of privacy settings, any written material (or photos) posted to a public medium (which the internet is, without question) *is* public. Suggestions about implementing more legislation to safeguard users, for example by preventing employers from checking prospective employees' online details without their express agreement, or preventing universities from checking on prospective students, is taking the law several steps too far. Some people would say that the best mantra is to think twice before posting anything that you wouldn't be happy for your grandma to read.

Other organisations are more tolerant of Facebook and other social networking sites, and some actively encourage their use at work and even have their own company site on Facebook, specifically for employees only. We'll come back to this point again later.

I'm a committed Facebook/MySpace/Bebo user – What are my options?

Well, we think you have a couple. If you want to continue to use social networking sites just for social networking (and continue to upload risqué photos of you and friends on holiday or at parties for example) then you really do need to restrict access to your profile to just your friends. This means that if a prospective employer comes searching for information about your private life, even if they're a Facebook member they won't find anything except your profile photo and those of some of your friends. One word of caution here. If you're merely in a race to grow your tally of Facebook friends into the hundreds or thousands as soon as possible, you could end up friends with people who won't keep your profile, personal details and comments to themselves. So if, after a particularly hard day, you criticise your employer, your colleagues or your professor to your Facebook friends, can you count on them not passing this information on? It has been suggested that even if you change your information and photos, they may remain available for the world to see long after you've deleted them, due to the way that information gets 'cached' on the internet. However, we believe that this is a far smaller risk than not managing your privacy settings correctly in the first place.

You should also be aware of the risk of online identity theft, whereby your identity can be 'stolen' lock stock and barrel, and used by someone else. The reasons for this are many and varied, and range from mischief-making to crime, and it appears to be a growing phenomenon. In 2009, a fraudster set up a bogus Facebook profile of the Guyanan President, Bharrat Jagdeo, and collected almost 200 friends before the profile was taken down. It's not clear what the impersonator's aim was, but they have not been caught. In early 2008, a Moroccan computer programmer called Fouad Mourtada was not so lucky. In January of that year, he had set up a bogus profile on Facebook, claiming to be Prince Moulay Rachid, the brother of Morocco's King Mohammed VI. Mourtada said he did this for a joke, but the Moroccan authorities didn't see the funny side, and he was jailed for 3 years and fined $1,300[28.] Fortunately for Mourtada he was released by royal pardon in March 2008.

And it's not just the celebrities whose profiles get stolen. There are plenty of examples of ordinary members of the public who have fallen victim. Take Amol Rajan, the sports correspondent for the UK's Independent newspaper. In 2008, someone with a personal vendetta against him set up a profile in Rajan's name on Facebook, complete with details about his sexuality, relationship status, religion, political views and date of birth. The fraudster even went about contacting and making friends with people that Rajan had deliberately avoided. Eventually Rajan got Facebook to remove the profile, but he said that four more fake profiles, each one subtly different to the last, appeared on Facebook in the following months[29]. Also in 2008, the British media reported that a

[28] http://news.bbc.co.uk/1/hi/world/africa/7258950.stm

[29] http://www.independent.co.uk/life-style/gadgets-and-tech/news/how-a-fraudster-stole-

businessman called Matthew Firsht was awarded a total of £22,000 in libel damages by the UK's High Court after an ex-school friend set up a fake profile of him on Facebook, misused his personal information and made highly damaging allegations about his financial affairs, including that he owed money and avoided paying debts by lying[30].

In some parts of the world, online identity theft, such as setting up fake Facebook profiles, is being taken very seriously. In Australia, for example, the authorities are introducing laws which will allow the police to charge Facebook fraudsters for improperly accessing or using information without having to wait for them to steal money[31]. Although the internet is a public medium, you can help yourself by taking your privacy seriously. We'll talk in more detail about privacy, and how you should protect it, in Chapter 2.

Action:

The golden rule here is to actively manage your privacy settings, and be aware that they vary from site to site.

- Double check your settings to make sure they do what you think they do.
- Use the function 'view my profile as others see it' to check what can be accessed.
- Don't publish information that could make you the target of online criminals, such as your date-of-birth, address or phone number.

---

my-identity-on-facebook-876804.html

[30] http://news.bbc.co.uk/1/hi/uk/7523128.stm; http://www.independent.co.uk/news/uk/home-news/victim-awarded-16322000-over-libellous-profile-876803.html; http://technology.timesonline.co.uk/tol/news/tech_and_web/article4389538.ece; http://www.guardian.co.uk/technology/2008/jul/24/facebook.privacy

[31] http://www.dailytelegraph.com.au/news/national/facebook-identity-theft-enough-for-jail/story-e6freuzr-1225748436706

And as an employee, you should either abide by your company's Facebook policy or put together a business case for changing it (see the IBM Beehive case study below). If you do your own thing, and use Facebook during working hours against company policy, don't be surprised if you end up facing a disciplinary hearing. We suggest that if you don't like their position on social networking, you look for an employer who loves Facebook as much as you do.

I want to take advantage of social networking sites to enhance my public profile – What are my options?

If, on the other hand, you want to use your social networking profile to your advantage with future employers (or college/university) then you should make sure that it reflects the kind of employee, professional person or student that they want to see. So the photos, what you write, and what groups you join should all be consistent with the image that you want to portray. As one *Times* reader put it, it's no good posting a photo on Facebook of you apparently attacking a policeman, tagged 'kill the pigs', and then expecting to get a job with a law firm![32]

Action:

For now, here are five simple things you can do to start managing your public profile.

- Make sure any photos you upload are appropriate. As first-life etiquette experts, Debrett's, suggest in their guide to online etiquette, if you don't want to see it in your local paper, don't put it online[33].
- De-tag yourself from others' photos if necessary.

[32] http://technology.timesonline.co.uk/tol/news/tech_and_web/article3613896.ece
[33] http://www.telegraph.co.uk/science/science-news/3357556/Debretts-guide-to-online-etiquette.html

- Join groups that present the impression that you want to give.
- Don't write comments either on your profile, on your friends' walls or on groups that you may later regret (like email).
- Be careful who you friend. You don't have to accept all requests for contact.

In Chapter 4 we'll cover impression management in more detail.

The changing nature of social skills

For many years research has shown that effective interpersonal skills are essential for the formation of strong social relationships, which in turn improve our psychological well-being, and that poor social skills, the inability to make friends and loneliness and depression are also linked. So you might assume that, since using ICT like social networking increases communication between people (email, instant messaging (IM) and mobile texting, chat rooms and so on), that it has an overall positive effect on your social skills and therefore on your psychological well-being.

Early research, however, identified what was dubbed 'the Internet Paradox'[34] i.e. that increased communication via the internet actually had a negative effect. As a result, parents particularly have become concerned that their children's social skills, especially those needed for face-to-face interactions, are actually being eroded by using the internet. The *Times Online* reported that a "charm academy" is being created for IT students in response to employer complaints that too many lack basic social and business skills'.[35]

Fortunately more recent studies suggest that the link between

[34] Kraut, R., Kiesler, S., Boneva, B., Cummings, J., Helgeson, V., & Crawford, A. (2002). Internet paradox revisited. Journal of Social Issues, 58(1), 49-74.

[35] http://business.timesonline.co.uk/tol/business/career_and_jobs/article2518124.ece

ICT, social skills and well-being is not that straightforward; internet-use does not affect everyone in the same way – it depends on individual differences and the impact will depend to a great extent on your goals and motivations for using it.[36]

For example, Robert Kraut and colleagues at Carnegie Mellon University, USA, refer to one early study amongst families in Pittsburgh where it was found that extraverts who used the internet extensively were less lonely than those who rarely used it, whilst introverts who used the internet extensively were more lonely. It was also found that the internet increased the amount of communication between people but at the same time increased their stress levels. More recent studies only confirm that the jury is still out. One study amongst adolescents[37] suggests that online communication such as Instant Messaging actually stimulates wellbeing, rather than reducing it, however this doesn't mean that teenagers should chat online to their hearts' content. Researchers have also shown that the use of online instant communication applications, in particular IM and chatting, is related to compulsive internet use[38], and that brings a whole host of additional issues[39].

In terms of ICT use at work, in a study of office workers in California[40], it was found that greater use of email did not result in a significant decrease in actual social, verbal and non-verbal communication skills, although it made a difference to the individual's perceived social skills. So it's difficult to say conclusively that using the internet and social networking sites is having a

---

[36] McKenna, K., & Bargh, J. (2000). Plan 9 From Cyberspace: The Implications of the Internet for Personality and Social Psychology. Personality & Social Psychology Review, 4(1), 57-75.

[37] Valkenburg, P.M. & Peter, J. (2007). Online communication and adolescent wellbeing: Testing the stimulation versus the displacement hypothesis. *Journal of Computer-Mediated Communication, 12,* 1169-1182.

[38] van den Eijnden, R., Meerkerk, G., Vermulst, A., Spijkerman, R., & Engels, R. (2008). Online communication, compulsive internet use, and psychosocial well-being among adolescents: A longitudinal study. *Developmental Psychology*, *44*(3), 655-665.

[39] Caplan, S. (2007). Relations among loneliness, social anxiety, and problematic Internet use. *CyberPsychology & Behavior*, *10*(2), 234-242.

[40] Madrid, J., & Wiseman, R. (2003). Computer-Mediated Communication, Social Skills, and Loneliness. *Conference Papers -- International Communication Association*, Retrieved January 27, 2009, doi:ica_proceeding_11316.PDF

negative impact on interpersonal skills generally; it would seem that this may only be the case for some people. What is undoubtedly true, however, is that ICT is changing the way we communicate, as individuals, employees and consumers, as well as changing the way organisations work.

Companies such as Intel and Deloittes[41] have become so concerned about the way ICT has impacted how employees communicate that they've taken the drastic step of declaring 'email-free days' in an attempt to get their staff to talk more to each other, preferably face-to-face. One of us used to work at a large consulting firm where it was common practice to email colleagues sitting at the next desk rather than speak to them, the theory being that it was less disruptive to them and others in an open plan office.

The importance of social skills in the workplace

As the extract from the *Times Online* article above illustrates, ask any employer what skills they most value in their staff and they'll probably tell you it's not so much their technical know-how but their social skills, i.e. their ability to get on with other people, communicate effectively, manage conflict constructively and work as a team. Knowing how to collaborate with your colleagues, to influence, persuade and negotiate successfully are core interpersonal skills without which you won't get off the starting blocks in most organisations these days. Several reasons why social skills are increasingly important in an organisational context have been put forward:

---

[41] http://news.bbc.co.uk/1/hi/technology/7049275.stm

Pollar, O. (2000, March). Does email help or hinder at work? Using the electronic tool wisely will help make it efficient. The Orange County Register, sec. At Work Extra. P.9.

Walther, J. B. (1992). Interpersonal effects in computer-mediated interaction: A relational perspective. Communication Research, 19, 52-90.

Walther, J. B. (1993). Impression development in computer-mediated interaction. Western Journal of Communication, 57, 381-398.

Teamwork

The growing importance of teamwork in Western workplaces can be largely attributed to the success of Japanese management practices in the 1970s and 1980s (popularised in the West by the American professor W. Edwards Deming), which emphasise co-operation, trust and sustaining long-term relationships over the merits of individual performance, the more common workplace practice in America and Europe.

Project-based work

The way work is organised at the beginning of the 21st Century is very different to how it was organised twenty years ago. Think about how many different projects are on the go in your workplace at any one time or how many you have personally been involved in during the past year. It's true that many jobs can only be done by teams, making co-operation and collaboration with others essential. This helps to explain why effective project management skills have become so important in business these days too, and why there is increasing interest in the collaborative capability of Web 2.0 technologies.

Organisational 'Glue'

Psychologist and Professor of Management Ed Schein[42] argued that interpersonal relationships are the 'glue' which holds organisations together; as far back as 1983 he suggested that the successful implementation of new initiatives relied, not on systems or processes, but on *people*. In the intervening two and a half decades, the increasing speed of change in the workplace, and the number of new initiatives which get implemented on a project basis only serve to amplify the importance of good social and communication skills. Additionally, common sense tells us that social skills make or break our relationships with other people; and there is a huge body of

[42] Schein, E.H. (1983) SMR Forum: Improving face-to-face relationships. Sloan Management Review, Winter, 43-52.

academic research in the psychology and sociology fields which supports this.

More opportunities for human interaction

Largely facilitated by new technologies, companies are now connected to the outside world in many more ways than previously. According to the latest UK National Statistics available[43], approximately seven out of ten businesses have a website, and an increasing number also have blogs. They have automatic interfaces with customers and suppliers, for example for ordering and shipping goods. There are literally thousands of consumer-led forums and personal blogs on the web which tell the world what people really think of their products or services[44]; in fact, the success of many internet-based services (think EBay and Amazon) is founded on the principle of giving feedback to the product or service-provider. Rather than decrease the opportunities for personal interaction with stakeholders, technology has increased them, so much so that new business functions have appeared such as 'customer relationship' and 'business interface' managers. So, ICT has not done away with the need for interpersonal skills, rather it seems to have increased it, and made it more complex.

There has been a partial move away from the complete automation of all business processes, especially those which involve the end-user or consumer. Taking the UK banking industry as an example, in the 1990s the banks made a huge effort to automate everything and reduce costs by closing branches, and moving staff into low-cost call centres, many of which were also off-shored in places like India where labour costs are much lower. But this has only worked up to a point. Sometimes, customers actually need to speak to someone in the business face-to-face. Personal contact really matters. NatWest Bank has differentiated itself for many years using the advertising slogan 'Another Way', which emphasised the fact that they opened branches when other banks closed theirs and off-shored customer contact to call centres.

[43] http://www.statistics.gov.uk/pdfdir/ecom1108.pdf
[44] www.yourcompanysucks.com

Psychological well-being

Last but not least, robust personal relationships are essential to your psychological well-being. Before you ask 'what's that got to do with work?', there is a growing body of scientific research which suggests that happy people are more productive than unhappy people (as well as being more successful, more generous, more sociable and earning more money).[45] No doubt you'll have heard ex-colleagues say that the key thing they say they miss about work is 'the people'. Being with other people and being able to get on well with them is crucial to our health and happiness. In one study of college students[46] it was found that the key difference between the happiest 10% of the group and the rest was that the former had rich and satisfying relationships. They also spent the least time alone and the most time socialising, and were rated highest on good relationships by themselves and by others.

You may also hear employers and HR staff talking about 'emotional intelligence' (EI or EQ), a concept created by psychologists Mayer and Salovey[47] in the 1980s and popularised in business circles by Daniel Goleman in the 1990s[48]. Emotional intelligence covers areas like self-awareness, self-management, social awareness and managing relationships. In other words, some say, old wine in new bottles. Goleman has claimed that EI accounts for approximately 90% of star performers' success in leadership, but others are more sceptical. For one thing, having a high level of EI cannot make up for a lack of technical skill. And of course it depends on the relative importance of EI to performance[49]. The level of EI

---

[45] Lyuobomirsky, S, King, L. & Diener, E. (2005) The benefits of frequent positive affect: Does happiness lead to success? Psychological Bulletin, 131(6), 803-855.

[46] Diener, E. & Seligman, M.E. P. (2002). Very happy people. Psychological Science, 13(1), 81-84.

[47] Salovey P. & Mayer, J.D. (1990) Emotional intelligence. Imagination, Cognition and Personality,9, 185-211.
http://www.unh.edu/emotional_intelligence/EI%20Assets/Reprints...EI%20Proper/EI1990%20Emotional%20Intelligence.pdf

[48] Goleman, D. (1997) Emotional Intelligence: Why it can matter more than IQ. Bantam Books

[49] WOODRUFFE, C. (2001) Promotional intelligence. People Management. Vol 7, No 1, 11 January. Pp26-29.

required will vary depending on the task, the job or even the profession. Doctors, nurses, teachers and others in the health and education professions, for example, need far higher levels of EI than people who work in very technical fields such as computer programming, for example. That said, there is no doubt that a lack of 'people' skills could hamper performance in the workplace, regardless of role. The reason is that the higher up corporate ladder you climb, the more likely you are to have to manage other people, and deal with office politics, so your ability to manage relationships is crucial.

Social skills equal employability

The Confederation of British Industry, in their 2007 report 'Time Well Spent'[50], sponsored by the then Department for Education and Skills, believes that these interpersonal, communication and 'emotional intelligence' skills are so important to business success that they make the difference between you being employable and unemployable. This is partly why the UK government is so keen to start teaching them in primary schools, in the form of the Social and Emotional Aspects of Learning (SEAL) curriculum.

Why now?

At this point you may be wondering why social skills (or more precisely, the lack of them) have suddenly become such an issue in the workplace. Haven't they always been important to business and individual success? Well, going right back to where we started this chapter, the answer is partly to do with the fact that businesses are now competing globally, and the UK's performance has been pretty mediocre. The Leitch Review of 2006[51] identified the prospect of the UK's long term decline in global markets due to its lack of skills

[50] http://www.cbi.org.uk/pdf/timewellspent.pdf

[51] LEITCH, S. (2006) Prosperity for all in the global economy: world class skills: final report. Norwich: The Stationery Office. Available at: http://www.dcsf.gov.uk/furthereducation/index.cfm?fuseaction=content.view&CategoryID=21&ContentID=37

versus competing countries. The Chartered Institute of Personnel and Development's (CIPD) 2008 Learning and Development Survey of 729 UK organisations identified a particular concern around employability skills:

> *'The key skills that employers class as very important include interpersonal (79%) and communication skills (68%). However, 66% of organisations feel that new employees currently lack both communication/interpersonal skills and management/leadership skills. Yet, these are also the same skills that organisations feel will be required to meet business objectives in the future.' (p2)*

Linked to this, a further reason is the focus on diversity. The UK workforce is more diverse than ever before; the ability to communicate and get on well with all sorts of people from all sorts of cultures is more important than ever.

What is social networking? The power and potential

Wikipedia lists over 130 different social network sites[52], some general ones like Facebook , others more specialised like Last.fm (music), Skyrock (for French speakers), and CouchSurfing (hospitality exchange). Facebook and MySpace are the most popular, ranked 4th and 11th in the world based on the total volume of internet traffic generated. Academic research suggests that social networking sites are more about staying in touch with people with whom you already have offline ties rather than connecting and making friends with new people[53]. One recent study explored university students' use of Facebook and social capital, i.e. the

[52] http://en.wikipedia.org/wiki/List_of_social_networking_websites

[53] Ellison, N. B., Steinfield, C., & Lampe, C. (2007). The benefits of Facebook 'friends:' Social capital and college students' use of online social network sites. Journal of Computer-Mediated Communication, 12(4), article 1 http://jcmc.indiana.edu/vol12/issue4/ellison.html ; Lampe, C., Ellison, N. & Steinfield, C. (2006). A Face(book) in the crowd: Social searching vs. social browsing. Proceedings of the 2006 20th Anniversary Conference on Computer Supported Cooperative Work (pp. 167-170). New York: ACM Press.

various resources which accrue as a result of a relationship, such as useful information and emotional support. It found a strong connection between Facebook use and social capital, particularly 'weak ties', i.e. the loose bonds between individuals which provide useful information (such as employment connections), rather than emotional support. Additionally, the research found that Facebook helps people maintain relationships when they move from one offline community to another (such as moving from home to University). This tends to contradict popular press reports which suggest that Facebook and other social networking sites generally have a detrimental effect on existing face-to-face relationships. Additionally, the study found that Facebook usage contributed to psychological wellbeing, suggesting that it might provide greater benefits for users with low self-esteem and low life satisfaction. The study concludes 'online interactions do not necessarily remove people from their offline world but may indeed be used to support relationships and keep people in contact, even when life changes move them away from each other'.

How organisations are benefitting from Social Networking

From an organisational perspective, there are many benefits to be found in using the new collaborative web 2.0 technologies like social networking sites and forums to interact with existing, potential, and in many cases, *ex*-employees. Rather than allow the use of Facebook at work, some organisations have gone one step further by creating their own company social networking site, such as the IBM's Beehive (see Case Study below). The Siemens Scholar Network[54], like Facebook, allows users to create their own profile page and blog, to stay in touch with other "scholars", receive up-to-date information news about the company, find out about relevant events and find new job opportunities within Siemens.

[54] http://alumni.siemens-foundation.org/

IBM's Beehive Case Study[55]

Social networking via 'Beehive', the Big Blue's own corporate Facebook, is just one of the many uses of Web 2.0 technologies that the company has embraced. Like Facebook, Beehive allows users (aka 'bees') to

- create a profile
- share photos
- share social activities
- post updates & comments
- organise events
- tag others' photos
- track friends

But one of the key uses of the Beehive is to spark innovation through the creation of Top 5 Lists (called 'High5s': think Amazon's 'Listmania'). The idea is that users can compare lists, share opinions on subjects, in some cases prompting new ideas and in others, arriving at a 'definitive' list collectively.

Not surprisingly, new users are called 'new bees'. By accumulating points for activities like posts, comments, and photos, new bees grow into working bees, busy bees, and finally super bees.

Says Liam Cleaver, Program Director, IBM Jam Program Office (Office of the CIO) 'One of our goals is to create a 'smaller' company in spite of our size...Beehive has done more than anything than create a sense of community at IBM.'

In another case[56], T-Mobile, the UK network owned by Deutsche Telekom AG, set up an internet forum to enable its graduate intake

[55] www.intranetblog.com

[56] CIPD podcast episode 22 (July 2008). Social networking, recruitment and HR

to keep in touch with each other (and with T-Mobile itself) throughout the recruitment process, and also to keep in touch once they started work. According to Julia Porter, T-Mobile's Senior Recruitment Manager, the company benefited from this internet forum in a number of ways, both financially and non-financially: not only did it succeed in retaining 100% of its graduate intake, the networking continued cross-functionally once the graduates joined, thus enabling them to start their careers at T-Mobile with a ready-made support network.

Our fourth example is the Tennessee-based Krystal fast-food chain, which has been using social network sites for the past three years to interact with its consumers. It has a typical corporate website yes, but it also has pages on Facebook and MySpace and a company run video-site called thebigredcouch.com[57]. The company's home page also allows visitors to click through to several more sites which encourage interaction. Brad Wahl, Krystal's marketing VP, states that the 'No.1 objective is to engage the consumer with the brand and give them a reason to choose it over another brand'.[58]

And in December 2008 it was reported that the giant food and drink company Kraft is using Facebook marketing to enhance its socially-responsible image[59]. If users download an application called 'Kraft Supports Feeding America on Facebook' and convince their friends to do the same, the company will donate meals through the Feeding America charity – according to *Media Week*, in just two weeks this had led to a donation of 1.4 million meals.

Individual uses of Social Networking

As mentioned above, academic research[60] into social networking

[57] http://www.thebigredcouch.com/

[58] Farkas, D. (2008). Social skills. Chain Leader,13(11),38-39.

[59] http://thevibe.socialvibe.com/index.php/2008/12/27/earn-125-points-feed-the-hungry-on-facebook-with-kraft-and-feeding-america/

[60] Boyd, D.M., & Ellison, N. B. (2007). Social network sites: Definition, history, and scholarship. Journal of Computer-Mediated Communication, 13(1), article 11. http://jcmc.indiana.edu/vol13/issue1/boyd.ellison.html

usage has found that the primary goal of most people participating in sites like MySpace, Bebo, Facebook and so on is *not* to network, in the traditional sense of meeting and making connections with new people. Researchers claim that what most participants use these sites for is just to hang out. It's a space to communicate with existing friends, follow their movements, and let them know what you're up to, as well as a space which is away from their parents (or so they hope! – see below). The fact that you can see your friends' networks might enable new connections to be made, but this is not the primary goal of most people who have their profile on a social network.

As the UK's Office of Communications has pointed out, a great deal of the social networking research which has been carried out so far is based on US samples. In April 2008 Ofcom published its own research[61] defining five distinct types of social network user, which gives a slightly different picture of UK users.

Category	*Age*	*Gender*	*Uses Social Networks for...*
Alpha Socialiser	25	Male	Flirting, meeting new people, entertainment
Attention Seeker	n/s	Female	Getting attention by customising their profile and posting photos
Follower	All	Both	Keeping up with what friends are doing
Faithful	20+	Both	Rekindle old school/university/work friendships
Functional	Older	Male	Any specific, single objective

This categorisation has been quoted in various highly respected market research forums; on the downside, it's worth being aware that the research was carried out using a very small number of users!

[61] http://www.ofcom.org.uk/advice/media_literacy/medlitpub/medlitpubrss/socialnetworking/summary

The downsides – your electronic footprint

Even if you just use Facebook or MySpace to hang out with friends, and are not intent on using it actively to promote your career, you need to be aware that, depending on the site and the privacy settings you choose, it may be possible for members of the public, and that includes current and potential employers and universities, to view your profile and postings. And although you might adjust the privacy settings so that only your friends can see your profile, you should be mindful that anything posted on a network site (text or photos) might come back to haunt you, and sooner than you think.

Living your private life in the public arena

- According to media reports, in November 2007 American intern Kevin Colvin emailed his boss at the Anglo Irish Bank saying that he needed time off because something had 'come up at home in New York', when really he just wanted to go to a Halloween party. His boss decided to check out Colvin's Facebook page and came across photos of him dressed as a fairy at the party the night before. To his complete embarrassment, Colvin's boss emailed him back, including a copy of the fairy photo, and copied in everyone else in the company.
- In February 2008 Inspector Chris Dreyfus, head of royalty and government protection for British Transport Police, had his promotion to Chief Inspector withdrawn by Bedfordshire police. It was discovered that he had posted intimate details about his gay lifestyle and suggestive comments to other users on Facebook[62]. Dreyfus had been

[62] http://www.telegraph.co.uk/news/uknews/1580094/Inspector-loses-promotion-over-Facebook.html

asked to remove the details from Facebook by his managers, but hadn't done so.

- According to *Personnel Today* magazine, in February 2007 UK retailer Argos sacked one of its employees for gross misconduct after he posted derogatory comments about the company on Facebook[63]. How Argos got to hear about the posting was not revealed.
- In July 2009 it was reported[64] that in Iowa, USA, a 27-year old reserve police officer, Abigail L Keller, was forced to resign over suggestive pictures of herself she had posted on her MySpace page. 'In this technology age, she used poor judgement when she posted these pictures in albums on her social network pages and naively believed no one but close personal friends could access these pictures,' said Administrative Law Judge, Debra L. Wise.
- In the UK in July 2009, the wife of Sir John Sawers, the next head of MI6, the overseas secret intelligence service, created a media furore after it was revealed that she had posted family holiday photos (including one of Sir John in a swimsuit) and their address details on Facebook[65]. Although the government tried to play it down, claiming that wearing Speedos was 'not a state secret', the incident was highly embarrassing.

Research[66] conducted by the Information Commissioner[67] in 2007

[63] http://www.personneltoday.com/articles/2007/08/08/41857/argos-sacks-employee-for-derogatory-facebook-entry-as-directory-enquiries-firm-118-118-asks-facebook.html

[64] http://www.desmoinesregister.com/apps/pbcs.dll/article?AID=/20090705/NEWS10/907050336&s=d&page=2#pluckcomments

[65] http://news.bbc.co.uk/1/hi/uk/8134807.stm

[66] http://www.ico.gov.uk/upload/documents/pressreleases/2007/social_networking_press_release.pdf

[67] http://www.ico.gov.uk/

suggests that up to 4.5 million (71%) 14-21 year olds would not want a college, university or potential employer to search for them on the internet unless they could remove content from social networking sites first. But almost 60% had never considered that what they put online now might be permanent, and accessible years into the future. Quotations from the young survey respondents themselves included:

- 'I think it is quite daunting as it could hinder my career choice' (female, 19, West Mids)
- 'Potential employers could 'google' you and it could give embarrassing information etc' (male, 16, NW)
- It sort of scares me to think that what I've written at my age now (17) may come back to haunt me in later years. I did not know this (female, 17, NW)
- 'Initial thoughts – who cares? Subsequent thoughts – omg!!!' (Female, 14, Scotland)
- Really annoying, a search on google brings up stuff I put online when I was really young and I can't get rid of it. (Male, 16, SE)

David Smith, Deputy Commissioner for the Information Commissioner's Office (ICO), said: 'Many young people are posting content online without thinking about the electronic footprint they leave behind. The cost to a person's future can be very high if something undesirable is found by the increasing number of education institutions and employers using the internet as a tool to vet potential students or employees.'

The ICO has even published their own top tips for protecting your privacy online, as well as setting up a website especially to support young people[68].

[68] http://www.ico.gov.uk/youth.aspx

ICO's Top Tips for protecting your privacy online

- A blog is for life: if you don't think you'll want it to exist somewhere in 10 years time, don't post it.
- Privacy is precious – choose sites that give you plenty of control over who can find your profile and how much information they can see. Read privacy policies and understand how sites will use your details.
- Personal safety first – don't allow people to work out your 'real life' location e.g. your place and hours of work. Your personal safety offline could be affected by what you tell people online.
- Password protected – change your passwords regularly, don't use obvious words like your pet's name and don't use the same passwords on social networking sites as you do for things like internet banking.
- Address aware – use a separate email address for social networking.

It has been suggested[69] that using what is effectively private information to make judgements about someone's ability in the workplace or in the tutorial group is discriminatory, and that employers and universities should not scour Facebook, MySpace or Google to see what they can find out about the private lives of potential or existing employees and students. Some in government have even tried to get a change in the legislation[70], such that employers would require permission beforehand. So far it's still legal practice, although the CIPD suggests that HR departments discourage managers from doing so, in case it's later seen as discrimination. Frankly, how this could be proved in a court of law, assuming it got that far, is anyone's guess.

[69] http://www.worksmart.org.uk/rights/not_appointed_because_of_facebook_profile
[70] http://technology.timesonline.co.uk/tol/news/tech_and_web/article3613896.ece

In short, it's probably safest to assume that anything you post anywhere on the internet, whether on forums or between friends on your favoured social networking site, is effectively in the public arena, and thus available to whoever wants to look for it. It's also worth remembering that good friends today may not be good friends in a year's time. We'll talk more about this in Chapter 4.

Individual uses of Social Networking – the upsides

According to the Pew Internet and American Life Project[71], social networking sites are becoming more popular among adults. Their report shows that approximately 75% of US adults use the internet, and of those 35% use social networking sites like Facebook, MySpace or LinkedIn. In just four years this number has quadrupled (in 2004 only 8% of adult internet users participated in social networking). If these growth rates continue, it won't be long before virtually everyone is active on social networks and has a public profile, and that could include your mum, dad and grandma!

Whilst research findings[72] that people mostly use social networking to 'hang out' may be true of the younger generation of social network users, it could be that the older generation of users are much more savvy about how to get the best out of such sites and utilise them in a much more active way. Indeed we would go so far as to say that if you aren't using social networks for more active networking, you're missing out on their potential to find new opportunities, make new connections and help you promote yourself and your career. In the next chapter we'll focus on how you can start to do this by exploring how to network using your online profile.

---

[71] http://www.pewinternet.org

[72] Boyd, D. M., & Ellison, N. B. (2007). Social network sites: Definition, history, and scholarship. *Journal of Computer-Mediated Communication*, 13(1), article 11. http://jcmc.indiana.edu/vol13/issue1/boyd.ellison.html

2

Networking in the Facebook Age

First things first

This chapter is all about getting social networks like Facebook, LinkedIn and Twitter to work for you. Whether you're an individual or a business, using social networking sites to raise your profile or strengthen your brand name is becoming more and more common. We take a very practical approach, covering the basic mechanics of how to create a social networking profile, drawing on relevant psychological research where appropriate. Although on the surface these three sites have different uses and attract different types of people, as we established in Chapter 1, more and more employers are using social networks to find out about prospective employees, and there is no reason why you shouldn't capitalise on this potential exposure by making sure that the profile you present to the public anywhere on the internet is attractive, interesting and engaging for them to read. Don't forget that space is limited on an application form or CV, so your social network profile could be the opportunity to fill in the gaps with attention-grabbing material. And no, we don't mean photos of you skiing down the slopes of Ben Nevis dressed as a chicken, unless these skills are called for in your line of work. But you can use your profile to highlight your talents, interests and expertise in ways that prospective employers or clients will value, and will want to follow up. But before we get into the detail of how to get set up on Facebook or LinkedIn, let's explore some of the concerns about internet and social networking use.

The psychological upsides and downsides

Interestingly, early research[73] into the psychological effects of internet use (before the advent of social networking) led to a great deal of negative media coverage, such as the New York Times front-page headline 'Sad, lonely world discovered in Cyberspace'[74]. Although the media response at the time was exaggerated, even today concerns persist that using the internet is somehow bad for human communication and social relationships[75]. This is sometimes referred to as the 'Internet Paradox', which is that a mainly social medium seems to have the opposite effect, causing people to become more socially isolated and lonely.

Subsequent research[76] shows that the picture is (unsurprisingly) more complex. The impact of internet use does vary from person to person, and is dependent, for instance, on psychological type. It seems that pre-existing differences between people are increased, the so-called 'rich get richer' hypothesis. So the Internet Paradox may only hold true some people. Extraverts, for example, tend to use the internet for social purposes, such as meeting new people and participating in chat-room discussions, so for them increased internet use can make them even more sociable.

Who are you on the Internet?

More recently, well-known UK psychologists have labelled social networking in particular as a bad for your psychological and physical health, much to the scorn of committed social network users. Dr Oliver James, quoted in the *Times*, said 'Twittering stems from a lack of identity. It's a constant update of who you are, what you are,

[73] Kraut, R. Patterson, M, Lundmark, V, Kiesler, S., Tridas, M. & Scherlis, W. (1998) Internet paradox: a social technology that reduces social involvement and psychological well-being? Amercian Psychologist, 53, 1017-31.

[74] NY Times, Harmon, 1998, cited in Joinson, A.N. (2003) Understanding the Psychology of Internet Behaviour. London, Palgrave Macmillan. p86.

[75] Aric Sigman paper 2009

[76] Kraut, R. Kiesler, S., Boneva, B., Cummings, J., Helgeson, V. & Crawford, A. (2002). Internet paradox revisited. Journal of Social Issues, 58(1), 49-74.

where you are. Nobody would Twitter if they had a strong sense of identity'[77] – even though, as far as we are aware, no research into identity and Twitter users has been carried out.

The concept of identity and its creation, maintenance and change, is one which has stretched the minds of great psychologists since the turn of the 20th century. It's largely agreed that identity is socially constructed, in other words, a product of our environment, upbringing and values. Not only that but online, we can choose to reconstruct our identities, consciously or subconsciously making ourselves appear more attractive. All of this creates further tensions between our authentic self and our constructed self.

Dr Aric Sigman, on the other hand, takes a biological perspective. He suggests that face-to-face interaction has beneficial effects on the physical body which are adaptive for human survival, and which don't occur when we communicate online. So his anti-social networking stance is extrapolated from this research, the theory being that time spent social networking is time which, prior to the invention of social networking, would have been spent in face-to-face contact The trouble is that unlike other human activities which are bad for us (binge drinking, over-eating, smoking to name but a few), we cannot physically see the effects of social networking. But on the plus side social networking is a relatively new phenomenon, and the way we use it is developing and changing. So for now we'd suggest that as long as you maintain your share of face-to-face relationships and avoid being constantly on the site waiting for the next communication, then they are useful tools.

So what has scientific research revealed about human communications, relationships and the internet which might help today's social network users? Let's take a step back here and start with the basics, concerning the power of online anonymity and reduced social cues, such as people's appearance, environment and non-verbal behaviour, and their effect on the way we communicate

77 http://women.timesonline.co.uk/tol/life_and_style/women/the_way_we_live/article5747308.ece

over the internet.

You may have come across the 'strangers on a train' phenomenon[78], whereby, people often reveal intimate details of their lives (details which even friends and family don't know) to complete strangers, usually because they believe that they'll never meet again. You may be surprised to learn that online, people generally do the same, that is they give away more about themselves than they would do in if they met the same person face-to-face. This has been shown in research on the effectiveness of medical consultations, where patients provided more detail about their personal and medical histories to a computer than if their GP asked them the same questions face-to-face[79.] In group activities, people who work together over the internet were significantly more socially-oriented than people who discussed the same tasks face-to-face[80], and anonymous internet groups disclosed four times as much information about themselves as groups which worked face-to-face.[81]

Interestingly, people reveal the most about themselves online when they can see themselves at the same time (for example they can see a photo of themselves on their profile page, or they can see themselves in a mirror) but can't see the person they're communicating with (for example, if their friend doesn't have a photo of themselves on their profile page). And even when they have a reasonable expectation of meeting the other person online again[82], they still feel relatively anonymous and thus are likely to disclose intimate details of their lives (the strangers on a train idea).

[78] Zick Rubin 1975 (Hamburger book p200)

[79] Ferriter, M (1993). Computer-aided interviewing and the psychiatric social history. Social Work and the Social Sciences Review, 4, 255-263.

[80] Walther (1995). Relational aspects of computer-mediated communication: experimental observations over time. Organisation Science, 6, 186-203.

[81] Joinson. A. N. (2001). Self-disclosure in computer-mediated communication: the role of self-awareness and visual anonymity. European Journal of Social Psychology, 31 (2), 177-92.

[82] McKenna, K.Y.A. & Bargh, J.A. (2000) Plan 9 from Cyberspace: the implications of the internet for personality and social psychology. *Personality and Social Psychology Review, 4,* 57-75. McKenna, K.Y.A, Green, A.S. & Gleason, M.E.J.(2002). Relationship formation on the internet: What's the big attraction? *Journal of Social Issues, 58,* 9-31.

This means that a close relationship can develop much more quickly than it would if you met the same person face-to-face. So you do need to be aware that, even if in 'real life' you're normally quite a reserved person, on the web it's much easier to give away private information about yourself that you wouldn't tell people if you met them in the flesh. You only have to look at someone's Facebook wall or Twitter stream to see what we mean. And whilst we don't want to be alarmist, revealing any private or intimate information, whether to friends or strangers on the internet, may come back to haunt you at a later date.

So now that we've talked about how easy it is to tell the world your innermost secrets unintentionally, let's get down to the business of how to set up a profile page. This is your personal 'home page', it's where you complete personal information about yourself such as name, date of birth, education and the groups you belong too, as well as your photo. LinkedIn and Facebook profiles are different, so we'll outline separately the information that you can show. Before we do any of that, it's worth considering what your networking goals are.

What is your networking goal?

Do you have clear ideas about what you want to achieve in using social network sites? For example, are you interested in a specific job in a particular industry and want to find people in those fields who can help you? Are you considering a complete change of career and looking for more information about the types of opportunities available? Do you want to find out what a particular career is really like before you make the leap? Or are you looking to get in touch with a particular person, because of their experience or skills? Whatever your purpose, it will guide your activities and behaviour on networking sites, so it's important to be clear about this first.

Do you want to:

- find people who are experts in particular fields – perhaps to ask for careers advice?
- start up new projects and find people who might be interested in collaborating with you?
- find potential business partners or investors?
- discover new opportunities in your professional field?
- keep track of who is being hired by whom?
- join professional groups?
- be introduced to potential clients?
- simply manage your public profile and enhance your reputation as a professional?

Depending what your aim is, you may find that you use social networking sites in different ways. So think carefully about what you want to get out of using social networking, and this will help you determine your goals clearly and concisely.

How to set your networking goals

So how do you determine what your goal is? Well, if you're already working, you may be very familiar with the whole process of goal-setting already, perhaps using the 'SMART' formula, or something similar. The SMART method, used to improve your chances of achieving your goal, can be applied just as successfully to the creation of personal goals as it can for work goals.

SMART Goals

Specific – Write down what you want to achieve in detail. Be as specific as possible. Use 1 Who, What, When, Where, Why and How questions to clarify the details.

Measureable – Make you goal measurable – how will you know when you have achieved your goal? What will you see, hear and feel on achieving it?

Achievable – sometimes people inadvertently set goals which are heavily dependent on other people – but in order for you to be able to achieve your goal, it must be within your own control.

Realistic – once you've slept on it, look again at your goal and double-check that it is realistic.

Time-bound – set a deadline for achieving your goal. Only you can decide when this should be, but it must be realistic, neither too soon, nor too far into the future.

In addition to making your goal 'smart', we would add two other important points.

Firstly, make sure your goal is stated positively. For instance, if you're trying to lose weight, you would state your goal as 'I want to be my ideal weight (whatever that is)' rather than 'I want to lose weight' (giving something up) or 'I don't want to be overweight' (stated in the negative). The reason for this is that the human mind cannot *'not'* focus on something. So if we say 'Don't think of a grey elephant', the first thing that will come into your head is a grey elephant! Therefore, you must give yourself a positive action to focus on.

Secondly, always consider the costs of achieving your goal. There will always be some disadvantages – these could be financial, to do with the amount of time and effort you will have to commit, or something else entirely. In the example of losing weight, you may have to commit time and money to attend a weight-loss class, a gym or take up a new sport. You may also have to deal with a friend's jealousy when you achieve your new streamlined figure. And you will probably have to spend money buying new clothes. So in order to be able to reach your goal, we recommend that you consider all the possible costs or drawbacks and think about whether you're prepared to accept them and work out a way to overcome them. In our coaching experience, in the excitement of setting new goals people frequently focus on the upsides and forget about the downsides.

Action:

- Spend 30 minutes setting your social networking goal(s), using the SMART method. Check your goal for i) positive voice and ii) costs/disadvantages. Ask yourself if you are willing to accept the costs.
- Review your goal(s) a day or so later. You may want to do this with a close friend whose opinions you trust. Ask them if it is realistic. If not go through the SMART steps again.
- Once you are happy with your goal ask yourself 'On a scale of 1 to 10, how committed am I to achieving this goal?'
- If you rate your commitment below 8 you are unlikely to really go for it. Ask yourself what needs to change to increase your commitment.
- Revise your goal if necessary.

Having set your networking goal, let's now run through the basics of setting up your profile page.

LinkedIn

How to set up your profile

First you have to register with LinkedIn[83] and provide some basic information, such as your name, email address, the company you work for and your work title. Then you need to create a profile; you can do this in stages if you want to, rather than complete the whole thing in one go. As you fill in your details in the various sections, the handy progress gauge on the right hand side reminds you how much you have left to do. But don't feel that you have to complete every section in full, it's entirely up to you how much information you disclose; you can leave some sections blank if you want to, or enter minimal information.

Near the top of your profile page, on the left hand side, your employment and education details will be summarised. Further down there is space to outline your professional experience and goals, and to describe your areas of expertise. What people write here varies enormously from person to person. Some make lists, write in bullet points or describe their experience in the third person in a fairly formal style, and others write whole paragraphs in the first person using a chatty approach. Some LinkedIn members use the space more creatively, adding testimonials, recommendations or appropriate quotations. All of these methods can be effective; it very much depends on your individual taste, the industry you work in and the audience you are trying to reach. Think of your profile as a kind of story about you – you want to make sure that all the pieces fit together, that people can see and understand the progress you have made in your career and how your career choices have made you the person that you are now.

[83] www.LinkedIn.com

Top Tips for defining and refining your LinkedIn Profile Summary

Write succinctly, and make every word count. Like readers of soft-copy CVs, readers of LinkedIn profiles haven't got the time to wade through a thousand word essay on why you chose to become a trademark lawyer or which societies you joined at University ten years ago. They want to know who you are, what you can do, and what you're aiming for in the future.

Choose your words carefully. Write about yourself positively of course, but there is a fine line between appearing confident and self-assured, and bragging unrealistically about your skills and achievements. You can polish what you have written at any time.

Although you can cut and paste chunks from your CV, avoid using clichés like 'a highly talented sales/marketing/finance professional with a proven track record in.....'. Whilst you don't have to come up with a Pulitzer Prize-winning summary, it's good to be original. Readers want to see something meaningful, not glossy words. If you describe your achievements shrewdly, we think your talent and track record will speak for themselves.

It helps to think of your Summary as a personal advert. In business this is sometimes referred to as an 'elevator pitch' (or as a Unique Selling Point, or USP), in other words your one minute summary of who you are, what you've achieved and what makes you distinctive. As we mentioned above, you can carefully craft a paragraph or two here which does make you stand out from the crowd, but without making you sound arrogant or overdosed on business jargon. Go easy on 'Buzzword Bingo' phrases like 'take it to the next level', 'best of breed' or 'bleeding edge'. These could sound trite to readers who will have seen them many times before.

The point of the Elevator Pitch is that it is concise, to the point and compelling; it gets your message across in the most appropriate way. The same should apply to your LinkedIn Summary. No one wants to read some rambling, incoherent piece. Most people talk at a rate of about 200 words a minute, which is about the limit you should keep to in your Summary section.

How to draft your one-minute advertisement:

Spend 15 minutes thinking about your most important and meaningful experiences and achievements. These may be to do with work, or with your life outside work.

Using a notebook or a Word document, describe each one in writing using the STAR method, which is an effective career-coaching technique:

- **Situation** – what was the situation/context?
- **Task** – what was the task you carried out?
- **Actions** – what actions did you take?
- **Results** – what were the results?

Do this for each of your main or most meaningful achievements.

When you have written a few sentences or a paragraph for each achievement, stand back and see what themes or patterns emerge from these examples. What was it that you cared most about achieving – for instance, was it good customer service, high quality production, product innovation, was it about developing other people or helping them achieve their potential? Was it about overcoming difficult challenges? Getting a team to work effectively together? Creating something new and original? What do these situations say about you as a professional and as a person?

Once you have identified some themes, spend some time reflecting on them. Do they ring true? Do they describe the real you? If you asked your friends and colleagues, would they choose those same themes to describe you, your interests or your style of working? Ask for feedback from friends and colleagues who know you well.

Pick the themes which best describe your interests and use them to showcase your achievements. Again, you can always ask close friends and colleagues to review your Summary before you post it online. Make sure you use the spellchecker.

Remember that you can edit your Summary at any stage. Once you have posted it online, go back to it after a day or so and see what it reads like from a distance. We recommend that you put aside regular time to spend on maintaining your LinkedIn profile, and that you always review it when you change jobs or achieve a major new goal.

Getting publicity for your achievements

Notice that you can change your Privacy Settings in LinkedIn so that your connections are notified when you make significant changes to your profile (and status), or you can prevent them from seeing the changes you make. Initially, you may want to prepare your profile in a Word document until you are happy with it before posting it online. Make sure your Privacy Settings are such that your connections can see any new updates that you make, such as when you change jobs or update your status. This way, it's very easy to keep all your contacts updated on your career progression and achievements.

How to check whether your connections automatically see your status updates:

Click on the Accounts and Settings menu at the top right hand side of your profile

Then under the Privacy Settings paragraph you will see an option for Profile and Status Updates. Here you can change whether or not your connections are notified.

If you decide not to notify your connections while you set up your profile, make sure you remember to switch this option back on once you have completed it!

The importance of recommendations

You can make your LinkedIn profile really stand out with some good quality recommendations, so you need to know how to request them. This may seem a bit daunting to start with. Having public endorsements may seem a strange thing to do, but this has been an increasingly common way for some business cultures, like those in the USA, where recommendations are almost mandatory.

In our experience, most people are only too glad to support trusted friends and colleagues, so providing your request for a recommendation is genuine (i.e. the person you're asking can honestly vouch for the quality of your work), they will be happy to help you. Most recommendations are only a few sentences or a paragraph long, so they won't take up a huge amount of time to write.

It has been suggested that because LinkedIn recommendations are public comments, they carry more weight than the usual work references. Hopefully you have a large number of connections in your network, and a fair number that you feel you can ask to endorse you. There's nothing stopping you asking the connections who worked for you too. In fact, having 360° endorsements will show that not only are you a high quality employee, but your peer group and the people who work for you rate you highly too. Decide which connections you are going to ask, and think about what role, skill or project you will ask them to recommend you for.

LinkedIn gives you the option of sending a 'standard' recommendation request, but this is a bit like sending a Christmas card with a pre-printed signature. It can give the impression that you don't think enough of the person to write to them individually. Writing a personalised request is more polite and also enables you to be specific. After all, if you've worked with someone for several years, there may be a number of different projects or roles they could comment on, so help them (and help yourself) by making your request as specific as possible.

How to create a request for a recommendation

Using the menu on the left hand side of the LinkedIn page, click on the 'Recommendations' option. If you cannot see it, expand the 'Profile' option by clicking on the '+' sign. Underneath you should see 'Edit My Profile', 'View My Profile' and 'Recommendations'.

Click on the 'Select Recommendations' tab.

In Step 1, use the down arrow to select the position that you want to be recommended for. You will see that the menu includes all the jobs you have entered on your profile page, including your student positions.

In Step 2, select the person you want to ask for an endorsement. Click on the LinkedIn icon on the right hand side to see a list of all of your connections presented in alphabetical order. Use the scroll bar on the right hand side to find the person you want to ask (or use the 'Narrow Your Connections' fields at the top), tick the box next to their name, then click on 'finish'. You can select more than one person, but this makes it more difficult to write a personalised note (see 5 below).

Step 3 already has LinkedIn's standardised text set out for you, but we advise you to delete it and personalise both your message and the subject line. For example, you could give your connection some further information about the job, project or experience you want the endorsement for. So rather than ask them to recommend you in your role as a Customer Relationship Manager (which encompasses many tasks) you could ask for a recommendation on your project management experience or your communication skills, mentioning a specific project you worked on together. This way, the recommendation will come across as being much more genuine (and useful to the reader) than a blanket 'John is a very professional Customer Relationship Manager' style response.

Click 'send'.

You can also access the 'Request Recommendations' page directly if you scroll down your profile page to the relevant job that you want a recommendation for. You will see at the bottom of that job section a link in blue. If you click on it, it opens up a new window.

Some LinkedIn guides suggest that the more recommendations you get the better, but we feel that they can be overdone. Few people have the time to read everything on your profile, and you will want your key successes to stand out. If you have scores of recommendations, the most important information may be swamped. Four to five endorsements should suffice. But, as we mentioned above, the US business cultures appears to favour higher numbers and bolder statements than maybe the UK or Europe.

Some important points about recommendations

At some point you may receive a recommendation that doesn't refer specifically to the skills you'd like to highlight, particularly if your initial recommendation request was vague. If this happens, you have the option to hide the recommendation from your profile. But this would be a bit of a waste of an otherwise valuable endorsement. When this happened to one of us, we went back to our contact, thanked them for their recommendation, and asked them for a replacement (see below). We politely explained exactly how we were trying to position ourselves and referred to the shared experience that we wanted them to comment on.

When you receive a recommendation from a contact it will show up in your LinkedIn and email inboxes. Go to your LinkedIn inbox (click on 'Inbox' on the left hand menu), then click on the subject line of the recommendation. From here you can read the full text of the recommendation. You now have the following choices:

Accept recommendation

If you want to accept the recommendation, you can either show it on your profile, or hide it. In other words, you have to select 'Show this recommendation on my profile' – it won't appear on your Profile Page until you do this.

You can also accept and hide the recommendation – this could be a temporary measure for example if you are changing careers, and the recommendation no longer reflects the skills and talents you want to publicise. You may also want to hide a recommendation if the business relationship has broken down, as sometimes happens. Remember that if you hide the recommendation, you can always show it at a later date. To do this, click on 'Recommendations' from the left hand menu. On the 'Received Recommendations' tab, scroll down to the relevant position where you can see how many hidden recommendations you have. By clicking on 'Manage, you will see the text of the hidden recommendation. From here you can show it on your profile by ticking the 'show' box. You also have the option to 'Request a new or revised recommendation' from your contact

Request replacement

As mentioned above, if the recommendation doesn't quite meet your needs you can use this option to ask your contact for a replacement. Again, LinkedIn provides a standard request, but we suggest that you write a personal message following the guidelines above.

Archive

The third option, to archive the recommendation, means that it will disappear from your LinkedIn inbox, but remember that you can always retrieve it and post it to your Profile Page at a later stage.

Education

The older you are, the less relevant your education history tends to be, unless you're a university academic by profession. What potential employers or clients want to see is that you have a good standard of education, but they're not necessarily interested in all the details of your qualifications, unless these are specifically relevant to the kind of job you do currently or the one you're looking for.

So if you're in your 30s and 40s or older, just list your University or College name, and the subjects you studied if they're relevant to the work you do. Very few people state their class of degree unless they gained a first, merit or distinction, although if you're younger, then it's more appropriate to include this information. The thing to remember is, if you're older, only include what is relevant to the role you have or the role you are looking for. Make sure that the education details you include help to explain your 'story'.

Photo

Choose a good quality head and shoulders photo, not a holiday snap of you on the beach in Bermuda, Bali or Bournemouth. LinkedIn photos are tiny, about the size of a passport photo, and unlike Facebook or Twitter, they don't expand when you click on them. So make sure you choose a clear face shot, avoiding too much background clutter which could be distracting.

So that was a quick tour through getting your LinkedIn profile set up, now let's turn to Facebook.

Facebook

How to set up your profile

With Facebook you also have to register first to get a Profile Page. The Facebook registration page[84] asks for your name, email address

[84] www.Facebook.com

and age. You can change your name once you have registered. Note that your first and last names are always shown on Facebook.

Facebook terms of service require you to enter your true date of birth; however, many people don't (see below). Once you have registered with Facebook, you can change the day and month of your birthday, but not the year. Facebook's profile options are very different to LinkedIn, which isn't surprising when you consider that it's aimed at social rather than business networking. Click on the Profile option from the blue menu at the top of the page, then click on 'Edit my profile', on the left hand side.

The profile page is made up of four sections

1. **Basic Information** – such as gender, date of birth, relationship status, religious and political views. You have to provide a date of birth to abide by the Facebook terms of service. There have been several cases in which users' profiles have been deleted by Facebook Inc for using the wrong date of birth or an alias rather than their real name. Of course, if you're using social networking to further your career, there's no point using an alias! But one of our colleagues, a social media consultant, advises clients never to use their real date of birth on any online networking site because of the risks (however small) of identity theft. Notice that you have the option not to show your date of birth on your profile page, or to show only the day and month. But your full date of birth details will still be accessed by any Facebook applications you use.

   The remaining areas in this section are voluntary and not relevant for a professional profile. So follow the advice of most experts in communications and leave the religion and politics boxes blank.

2. **Personal Information** – such as activities, interests, favourite music, TV programmes, books, films and quotations. Some Facebook guides suggest completing all of these sections with as much detail as you can think of, but we'd go for a more focused approach if you intend to use Facebook for more serious job-

related networking. If you're in the creative industry of course, telling everyone about your music, literary, TV and film preferences might be highly relevant. However there's nothing stopping you using some of these personal information sections to write about your career, achievements and development goals.

Top Tip

Ensure that what you write is coherent – it should provide a meaningful and compelling description of you and your career so far. Think about the 'story' that the information tells about you. Does it all hang together? You can write reams, or you can keep it short and to the point. Unless you're an engaging or accomplished writer, it's probably best to stick to 'short and sweet', using bullet points to keep you on track and to help guide your readers

3. **Contact Information** – here you can put your address, landline and mobile numbers, and the URLs for your website and/or blog if you have one. Notice that against each box is a lock symbol. If you click on it you can see you have the option to amend who can see these details, i.e. 'Friends of Friends', 'Only Friends', 'No-one' or 'Customise'. The customise option allows you to block certain named individuals. Think carefully about what information you show here, unless you know all your Facebook friends personally and know that you can trust them. If you're considering choosing the 'No-one' option (i.e. no-one but you can see your information), then simply leave these boxes blank instead.

4. **Education and Work Information.** Because Facebook started out as an application for students to keep in touch with each other on campus, your education information comes first. You can add more than one university and secondary school if appropriate.

Note that you don't have to show leaving dates, you can leave them blank. As we suggested above, the older you are, the less need there is to fill in lots of detail. Employers are not that interested in which school you went to ten or twenty years ago. The only benefit might be if you went to a prestigious school and/or one which has a strong alumni network.

As for work information, you can add as many jobs and employers as you wish. A description of your role, major projects or achievements could be helpful to friends and acquaintances. Some Facebook users and keen business networkers incorporate recommendations or testimonials in this space too. You can also include dates of employment, although this isn't mandatory.

Make sure that whatever education and work information you show here in Facebook ties in with the details shown on your LinkedIn profile.

Photo

If your goal is to use Facebook to network professionally, use a photo which matches the image you want to present. On LinkedIn you can only add one photo; on Facebook you can add hundreds, grouped into different 'portfolios'. So if you have photos of you in a work environment – presenting or speaking for example, you might like to add them. If you want to highlight your talent as a photographer though, we think that there are better websites to use.

Notice that clicking on a Facebook photo enlarges it considerably, so make sure that the one you upload is good quality. On LinkedIn we recommended that you stick to a head and shoulders shot, but on Facebook you do have more scope – you could upload a photo of something that represents you (for example, we've used a photo of this book). In fact, using a photo of something other than your face will make your profile stand out in the sea of other tiny face shots.

Video

Facebook also gives you the option of uploading a video –so you could post a clip of you presenting, speaking or training, or even a short video résumé. If the latter appeals to you, make sure it's well scripted and edited, not like the one created by the now infamous Yale student, Aleksey Vayner[85] and submitted to the investment bank UBS. Mysteriously entitled 'Impossible is Nothing', Vayner's video résumé, showed him skiing down mountains, karate-chopping bricks, ball-room dancing and playing tennis, all accompanied by a sound-track of his musings on self-development and how to achieve your goals. Unfortunately for Vayner, someone at UBS made the video public, and it has since become a Youtube classic on how not to apply for a job.

Setting up your Facebook profile page is quite simple, although the trick is to keep it fresh with new news about you, your activities and achievements and comments that others will find interesting. One of the ways to do this is to interact with your Friends regularly so that they comment on your Wall[86], and to keep posting new content and frequent status updates.

Concerned about privacy?

Facebook

Firstly, a few words of advice: read Facebook's Terms of Service (TOS) and Privacy Policy (which you can find links to at the very bottom of the page), particularly the sections 'Use of Information Obtained by Facebook', 'Sharing Your Information with Third Parties' and 'Third Party Advertising'. Think carefully about the personal information you disclose on your profile. In mid February 2009, Facebook attempted to change its TOS but had to revert to

[85] http://en.wikipedia.org/wiki/Impossible_Is_Nothing_(meme)

[86] A Facebook wall is the space on each user's profile page where friends can write messages and leave attachments for the user to see. A user's wall is visible to anyone with the ability to see his or her full profile,

the old ones after an outcry by certain savvy Facebook users and social media bloggers[87]. By late February, in a move designed to make Facebook more democratic and transparent, Facebook's founder, Mark Zuckerberg, announced that users would be able to have comment and voting rights over its future policies about how the site is run[88]

At the time of writing, the site's TOS Privacy Policy had not been updated since 2008, so we wait to see how new user comment and voting rights will operate in practice. At the moment they state that by registering, Facebook has the right to use your information, for example for the purpose of third party advertising, although it never identifies individuals to third parties. Additionally, 'Facebook may also collect information about you from other sources, such as newspapers, blogs, instant messaging services and other users of the Facebook service through the operation of the service (e.g. photo tags) in order to provide you with more useful information and a more personalised experience'.

Secondly, make sure that you are thoroughly familiar with the privacy settings on your Facebook account. You can access them by clicking the 'settings' menu on the top RHS of the page. Choose 'privacy settings' from the drop-down menu, and you'll find an overview page with four sections:

1. **Profile** – here you can control who sees your basic and contact information, and comments on your wall. On the Basic privacy page, each piece of information, with the exception of your profile and wall, has three options, 'Friends of Friends', 'Only Friends' or 'Customise'. You access these by clicking on the down arrow. The Customise option allows you to block certain friends from accessing your data. This might be useful if you have a competitor listed as a friend, for example. As well as the above three options, for your wall you can also choose 'Only Me' and 'No-one'. We have yet to work out a good use for 'No-one'! You

[87] http://blog.Facebook.com/blog.php?post=54746167130
[88] http://blog.facebook.com/blog.php?post=56566967130

can start to see that controlling your privacy on Facebook can get quite complicated if you haven't thought about it first.

When you have selected your settings, remember to click 'save' at the bottom. Notice that to check your privacy settings, you can view your profile as a friend would see it – put their name into the box at the top of the page and press return.

The other tab is for checking the privacy settings for your contact information. Some of you may be happy to share quite widely, but remember that all this information can then be accessed by the Facebook applications you use, as well as by application developers.

2. **Search** – here you can control how people search for you on Facebook. You can change your search visibility, alter the type of information that searchers can see (for example, whether they can see your photo, list of friends or the pages you're a fan of). Notice that you can also create a Public Profile. This is a useful tool if you want to increase the chances of a prospective employer or client finding you and want them only to retrieve certain information about you. Click on 'see preview' to check what information will be made public.

3. **Newsfeed and Wall** – note that stories will be published on the newsfeed and wall whenever you edit your profile information, join a new network or update your status. You can choose whether or not stories are also published when you do things like remove information from your profile, change your relationship status or write comments on a friend's wall. The default setting is that friends will be updated of your every comment and posting, unless you opt out, or unless you have blocked them using the profile privacy settings (see above).

4. **Applications** – when you install Facebook applications (such as SuperPoke! and Top Friends), they can access most of your information including the contents of your personal profile (e.g. work and education history), your photos and your wall, as well as your friends' personal info (depending on their privacy

settings). Additionally, applications that your friends use can access your information unless you change your privacy settings to prevent this.

To do this, go to settings> privacy settings>applications. You'll be faced with a page of text which has two buttons at the top left, 'overview' and 'settings'. Click on 'settings'. You will see a page entitled 'What Other Users Can See via the Facebook Platform'. You will notice that the default option is that ALL your information (apart from your contact details) can be accessed by applications (and thus by the people who develop them) that your friends use. If you want to retain some control over who can see your personal information, you may want to review these settings. Notice that you do not have the same level of control over the applications that you access in your own name. If you look at the applications>overview page, you will see that when you authorise a Facebook application, it will be able to access any information associated with your account that it requires to work. How this is decided in practice is not made public.

Facebook created another privacy controversy when it launched Beacon in 2007[89]. Beacon sends data to Facebook from external websites that users have visited, apparently to allow third party adverts to be more targeted and to allow users to share their activities elsewhere on the web with their friends, working on the assumption that you want to share *everything* you do online with all your friends, all of the time. Shortly afterwards, following some high profile campaigning[90] by pressure group MoveOn.org[91] Facebook announced that it had changed the Beacon system to an opt-in system, rather than an opt-out system.[92]

[89] http://www.facebook.com/press/releases.php?p=9166
[90] http://www.washingtonpost.com/wp-dyn/content/article/2007/11/29/AR2007112902503_pf.html
[91] http://civ.moveon.org/facebookprivacy/?rc=fb.privacysuccesspage
[92] http://blog.facebook.com/blog.php?post=7584397130

LinkedIn

When you join LinkedIn, you create a network of connections with other professionals and experts who you know and trust, because they're friends or people that you've worked with. In principle, you should only connect with someone that you know well enough to recommend. Whilst many LinkedIn members approach it as a competition (as in 'can I get more connections and recommendations than anyone else in my network?'), we'd suggest that the value of your network depends less on actual numbers than on what you do with it. If you never have any interaction with your connections once they're in your network, you're unlikely to be deriving much benefit from them.

LinkedIn's privacy policy

Like Facebook, LinkedIn shares your information with third parties such as advertising companies, but not in a way that makes you personally identifiable. When you sign up to use certain LinkedIn applications, your information is shared with the application developers, just as it is in Facebook You can opt out of 'web beacons' that is, having files on your profile which provide anonymous data to advertisers and target adverts at you. To do this, you need to go to the Accounts and Settings area, on the top right hand side of the page, then scroll down to the Privacy Settings section, click on Partner Advertising, and click on 'No'.

All in all, our take on privacy settings is that LinkedIn is simpler and easier to work with than Facebook for those using social networking sites for business networking. You don't get the option to block people in LinkedIn of course, but then on the basis that this is a professional network, you don't expect to have LinkedIn members lurking or making a nuisance of themselves anyway.

Twitter

Want to Twitter?

At this point, it's worth mentioning Twitter, a relatively new addition to the social networking scene. It is much easier and quicker to master than either Facebook or LinkedIn. Twitter is a micro-blogging service, which allows you to send very short messages (maximum 140 characters) to your readers from your PC, Blackberry or mobile phone. Twitter was launched in 2006, and was originally conceived as a means to update family, friends and contacts by answering the simple question 'What are you doing?'. Twitter users usually post their updates to the Twitterverse, where anyone on Twitter can read them, although there are options to send private messages to a specific Twitter user (see below for more information).

Once you've joined Twitter, and started following a few Twitter users you'll soon see that people have already begun to adapt it for a broader business and communications use. They don't tend to answer the 'What are you doing?' question anymore, instead they use their 140 characters to post links to interesting websites and blogs, snippets of news and gossip, expert opinions and basically anything that demonstrates their own talent and expertise in a particular field. It's another medium that can be used as a personal advert, and to drive traffic to your own website or blog, which is great news if you're in business, or wanting to impress potential employers or clients. The potential business benefits of using Twitter are such that the Twitter inventors have devoted time and effort to creating a special guide, complete with case studies and best practice, called Twitter101[93].

How to join Twitter

This is remarkably easy and much quicker than setting up a LinkedIn

[93] http://twitter.com/Twitter101

or Facebook profile. Just go to the Twitter website[94] and click on 'Join the conversation' to create your account. Choose your username carefully – since this is how you'll be known on Twitter. We're assuming that you want to use Twitter to generate interest, perhaps as an expert in your professional field or as a potential employee, rather than as a means to communicate with family and friends. So if you're already building up that kind of reputation, you may want to stick with your own name (if it's available). On the other hand, since your real name is always available to people if they click on your photo, you also have the option to create a brand-name instead: some people use a combination of their own name and that of their business or profession. Note that you can change your username later on, although you should let all your Twitter contacts know that you're doing this.

If you click on 'Settings' (top right hand side of the page) you'll find the area where you can change your username, enter your one line bio and your location. Note that your bio is only 160 characters long – a real test of your ability to write a succinct yet compelling elevator pitch. Have a look at what other people write in their bios. Play around with a few ideas, and try them out with people who know you well. You want to end up with something that is both clear and persuasive. Think of the key words that people searching Twitter for information (as journalists do[95]) will be looking for. The advanced search facility is tucked away at the bottom of the page.

How to 'follow' people, and acquire your own followers

When you 'follow' people on Twitter it simply means that you receive their Twitter updates (also known as 'tweets'). If they're following you, they'll receive yours.

On the top right hand side of the page you'll see a tab called 'find people'. If you know the Twitter username of the person you're looking for, or if they have an unusual name, it should be pretty

[94] www.twitter.com

[95] http://blogs.reuters.com/mediafile/2009/02/27/twitter-has-journalists-chirping/

easy to track them down using the 'Find on Twitter' tab. Once you've found them, simply click on their photo – you'll be directed to their profile page. Click on the 'follow' tab under their photo and you're now following them. If you know who you're looking for, it's very easy.

But if the person you're trying to find has a pretty common name, or you don't know their Twitter username, it may take you a little longer to track them down. Twitter gives you the option to search for people via other networks, such as Gmail, Hotmail and Yahoo, and you can also invite people you know to join Twitter if you know their email address. Hopefully with time, a more sophisticated people search function will be created.

Another other way to find interesting people to follow is by randomly searching tweets on the subjects your interested in – you can do this by using the advanced search facility, and searching on the key words or phrases that spark your curiosity. Once you've found some interesting comments, have a look at the user profiles and Twitter stream. It's pretty easy to see if they're likely to post similar material again. If you think so, you have nothing to lose by following them, and with any luck they'll follow you back. The likelihood is that the more followers you have the more you'll acquire, although the Twitter medium is too new to have any definitive answers on that score.

After a while you may find that you're following so many Twitter users that it's difficult to keep up with them all. You can either review your list and choose to stop following some (they won't be notified of this), or you can sign up for some Twitter software like Tweetdeck[96] to help you manage your incoming Twitterstream – for example by dividing the people you follow into subject groups.

How to 'Tweet'

You just type in your message (140 characters or less) and click 'update'. It's very simple. The art is in saying what you want to say in few words. If you're posting website links, use an application like

[96] http://tweetdeck.com

tinyurl.com, which shortens the URL and saves you space. You may find that you need a Twitter dictionary to get to grips with the jargon – there are plenty available online through Google.

To send a message directly to a specific person, rather than a general message to all your followers, type '@username' in the text box followed by your message.

If you want to reply to a message they have sent you, let your cursor hover over the right hand end of their message and a small upward arrow symbol appears; this is the 'reply to' function. Simply click on it and type your message.

Note that @ replies can be read by anyone who follows you or the person you're following.

If you want to send a private reply, you can use the 'direct message' function. Note that you can only send a direct message to someone if they are also following you. To send a direct message, simply type 'dm username' in the text box, followed by your message. Direct messages can only be read by the person to whom you are sending it.

Note that you can also delete a message you have sent if you change your mind. On your profile page, find the message you want to delete. Let your cursor hover over the right hand end of the message and two symbols will appear, a star (to mark it as a favourite) and a dustbin. Click on the 'dustbin' symbol and your message will be deleted from your profile page and from your followers' in-boxes. It's worth remembering that the deleted message may still appear for some time using the 'search' function, although if you've dropped a real clanger and want it to be removed urgently you do have the option of contacting Twitter Support (using the Help function) to get it removed. There's no guarantee that they'll do it quickly though, or do it at all!

A few words of advice on Twitter Etiquette – we hope that you'll only ever receive pleasant and welcome Tweets from your connections on Twitter, but there may come a time when you get critical feedback and feel tempted to respond in kind. We'd suggest that if this happens, you count to ten before replying. Don't forget that like all social networks, Twitter is a public medium, and your bio and messages can appear in a Google search. Twitter, like many other social networking sites, is still a relatively new area; 'social norms' are still being established for these spaces, so it's best to always err on the side of caution.

Twitter privacy

You can read anyone else's Twitter updates apart from those which are sent directly to another Twitter user using the direct message function. You can find specific people using the search function and go to their profile page to find all their public tweets. Naturally this means that unless you project your updates (see below) your Twitter stream is also available for anyone to read – they don't actually have to be following you.

You do have the option of protecting your updates, so that only friends and followers can read them. To enable this, go to 'Settings' (top right hand side of the page) and click on the 'Account' tab. Near the bottom of the page is a box labelled 'protect my updates' – if this box is ticked it means that people can only follow your status updates if you approve them. But if you're using Twitter as a way to publicise your professional knowledge and skills, then make sure your updates are not protected.

As mentioned above, you can use the 'direct message' option to send private messages to a specific person on Twitter if they're also following you. This gives you some measure of privacy. But we'd suggest that you don't rely on this remaining the case always and forever. There have been instances where Twitter privacy has broken down. For instance in April 2008 one Twitter user found that all her private direct messages appeared in her normal Twitter stream, so that anyone who logged onto her account could read them[97]. In fairness to Twitter, it was actually the fault of a third party application that the user had recently signed up for, not of Twitter itself.

This brings us back to the point we have made above – the

[97] http://www.techcrunch.com/2008/04/23/privacy-disaster-at-twitter-direct-messages-exposed/

internet is a public medium, and you shouldn't depend on it for sending private or confidential messages. Always think of the potential consequence of your message suddenly becoming available to everyone. And when it comes to using third party applications (in Twitter, LinkedIn or Facebook), as one Twitter user noted, 'If you give the keys of your house to strangers, don't be surprised when your stuff is gone'[98].

How many friends, followers or connections should I have?

Well, the short answer is as many as you can get, as long as you stay within the limits laid down by the particular social networking site. With LinkedIn of course, the idea is to re-create your actual work network, not make random connections to people you barely know, but with Facebook and Twitter, it seems that the more the merrier. At the time of writing these limits are as follows:

- Facebook Friends – 5,000
- LinkedIn Connections – 30,000
- Twitter Followers – no limit

Twitter doesn't have one set limit as such, it varies from person to person, based on your follower/followee ratio. It seems that they're less concerned about the number of people who follow you than the number you follow. This is to deter spam – so, for example, you can't follow 50,000 people, and only have two dozen following you.

Now you may be wondering why it's important to increase the size of your network beyond your normal circle of contacts. After all some Facebook and Twitter users have literally thousands of friends and followers.

As a rule we tend to think that strong ties (the type you have with close friends) are somehow better or more valuable than weak ties (the type you have with acquaintances). So the more time,

[98] http://tinyurl.com/laegkd

emotion, intimacy and so on involved in the relationship, the stronger the tie. And common sense tells us that it's highly unlikely that any one person can have a close relationship with hundreds of Facebook friends or Twitter followers. So what is the point of trying to extend the number of friends or followers that you have?

Well the 'strength of weak ties'[99,100] theory suggests that, paradoxically, weak ties can be more beneficial than strong ones, in some circumstances, for example when you are looking for a job. This is how it works. Our acquaintances move in slightly different social circles to us, and thus have access to different (and potentially superior) information and resources than our close ties (who move in the same circles as us) have, and so can provide us with a different (and potentially superior) kind of support.

So having a loosely-knit network of hundreds (or even thousands) of Facebook or Twitter connections based on weak ties is certainly not to be sniffed at, if anything it would make sense to use social networks to make as many connections as you can.

[99] Granovetter, M. (1973). The strength of weak ties. American Journal of Sociology, 78(6), 1360-1380.

[100] Granovetter, M. (1983). The strength of weak ties: A network theory revisited. Sociological Theory, 201-233.

3

Making the most of your networks and relationships

In this chapter we start by looking at the context of online networking. It's helpful to establish a few guidelines to help drive and focus your networking activities, whether these are online or face-to-face. In the previous chapter we asked you to consider your goals, i.e. what you specifically want to achieve through online networking. Now we will put those goals into context and encourage you to think about how you are going to achieve your goals and what exactly you will do. We will also cover some of the key ways to make the most of your online presence, such as joining groups and asking and answering questions.

Many of the business people we coach are a little uneasy or nervous at the outset about venturing into online networking. It's something that feels very much outside their comfort zone. We empathise, and are happy to admit that initially we too felt somewhat apprehensive. You might be concerned on a number of different levels: Are you presenting a professional image? How do you come across to others? Who else is out there? Are you setting up expectations which you cannot meet? It might seem as if other people are far more competent at online networking than you are. It's not surprising that it all feels a bit scary the first few times that you do it. It's human nature to compare yourself to others, who appear far more confident, well-connected and savvy than you.

However, we can say with certainty that you will quickly overcome your initial trepidation, and having clear goals about what you want to achieve, in sufficient detail that you know what a successful outcome is, really does help. Let's explore comfort zones in more detail now.

How to expand your comfort zone

'I am always doing things I cannot do. That's how I get to do them'.
Picasso

Comfort zones are curious things. They act as a survival mechanism, keeping us safe and protecting us from taking unnecessary risks. Stepping outside them makes us feel fearful, tense or panicky; being human, we try to get back inside our personal comfort zone as quickly as possible. But in order to grow and develop, we do need to take risks and try things we haven't done before. As babies we would never have learnt to walk and talk had we not done this. We accept there is the possibility that we may get it wrong (although there are always steps that we can take to minimise the risks). The important thing we want to get across to you is that your personal comfort zone can hold you back and can reduce the amount of learning experiences you have, unless you step outside it. In other words, you have to make yourself feel uncomfortable deliberately for new learning to take place.

Consultants who work in the field of personal and organisational change argue that reactions to change are frequently more emotional than rational. Frequently, they refer to the 'change curve', which is based on psychiatrist Elisabeth Kűbler-Ross's work in the 1960s and 70s on the human grieving process[101]. The change curve suggests that people go through a number of different active and passive emotional responses to a change they do not want, such as shock, denial, anger, depression, bargaining and acceptance.

[101] http;//www.ekrfoundation.org

Whilst there is very little empirical evidence to support it, the change curve has gained wide acceptance in organisations as a useful tool to help people understand and adapt to change.

A common mistake that people make is to assume that they need confidence in order to be able to achieve their goals. They say things like, 'When I'm confident, I'll be able to do that,' when in reality, they'll gain confidence from doing it, whatever 'it' is.

According to the work of psychologist Albert Bandura[102], one of the world's leading experts in the subject, self-confidence comes from four main areas:

- **Personal experience** – almost like trial and error, you keep going until you learn from your mistakes and get it right.
- **Vicarious experience** – watching or listening to someone else doing it, then modelling them. Learning a language is a good example of vicarious learning.
- **Persuasion** – when someone else actively encourages you and makes you feel as if you can do it.
- **Appropriate physiology,** e.g. feeling brave or psyched up and ready for anything.

This is why you sometimes hear coaches advise their clients to act the part, because merely by assuming the role of a confident person you can boost your self-belief – the 'fake it till you make it' phenomenon. We're not suggesting that you throw yourself into online networking with wild abandon; generally speaking a little forethought and preparation about what you're going to do when you get there is a good thing. What we're saying here is that you should expect to feel a little apprehensive at first, and welcome this discomfort as a sign that you have the opportunity to learn and develop. Through doing something new you will be expanding your comfort zone, and this in turn will increase your confidence. So, now that you are prepared to feel a little uneasy as you try online networking, what's stopping you?

[102] http://des.emory.edu/mfp/self-efficacy.html#bandura

Building trust online

My word is my bond

Online interactions are in many ways very different from face-to-face conversations, not least because you don't really know who you may be speaking to. This is compounded by other differences to face-to-face networking such as time-delay, and the lack of verbal and non-verbal social context cues. So you might expect that it takes longer to build up strong, trusting relationships on networking sites than it does offline. But as we mentioned in Chapter 2, the relative anonymity that you get online actually increases your propensity to self-disclose which in turns aids the trust-building process.

The simplest definition of trust from the field of psychology is 'confident positive expectations regarding another person's conduct'[103]. Trust is an essential part of any successful business relationship whether in the real-world or online. One theory is that trust decreases uncertainty about the future as well as reducing the effort in thinking about the consequences of someone taking advantage of you[104]. Social psychologists have identified various forms of trust, of which 'calculus-based trust' is the most relevant to networking. Calculus-based trust is built up quite simply on the basis of mutual support. If I help you and then you help me, trust can build up quickly between us. Another theory emphasises the deterrent effect more than the benefit, suggesting that the fear of harming your reputation by not acting in a trustworthy manner is a greater motivator than any potential benefit[105].

So how can we build trust quickly in online networking? It has been suggested that acting as if trust exists (i.e. trusting others even

---

[103] Lewicki, R.J., McAllister, D., & Bies, R. (1998). Trust and distrust: New relationships and realities. *Academy of Management Review, 23*(3), 438-458.

[104] Limerick, B. & Cunnington, B. (1993). Managing the New organization. San Francisco, Jossey Bass.

[105] Lewicki, R.J. & Bunker, B.B. (1996) Developing & maintaining trust in working relationships. In R.M Kramer, T.M Tyler & B Fairly (pp114-139).*Trust in organizations: Frontiers of theory and research*. Thousand Oaks, CA: Sage.

when you don't know that they can be trusted) swiftly leads to the creation of actual trust. In research into virtual business teams, those whose members were willing to show trust by committing themselves to the project from the start, by volunteering to take on work and going the extra mile themselves, even though they had no evidence that other team members would reciprocate, developed constructive, positive and trusting relationships much more quickly and were more successful as a result[106].

On a practical level, you need to be aware that online 'conversations' need more thought than face-to-face ones in which you have both verbal and non-verbal social context cues to help you interpret the situation. Take the time-delay for instance. In early research into computer-mediated communication, lag was primarily a technical issue which the advent of broadband has pretty much resolved. However, it is still perfectly possible for one person in an online chat, through MSN or Skype, to control the speed of their response in a way that is not possible in face-to-face conversation. Psychologists have suggested that synchronous chat (the type you get in chat rooms or when using instant messaging, versus the asynchronous chat of email) is acceptable when it falls reasonably close to a typical conversational lag[107], of between 1.35 and 3.21 seconds[108]. The fact that one party to the online chat can stop mid-conversation can be frustrating for the other party, who may be waiting for a response. You would never walk away from a face-to-face conversation and rarely from a telephone conversation without signalling your departure in some way, but it's much easier to do so online.

---

[106] Jarvenpaa, S., Knoll, K. & Leidner, D.E. (1998). Is anybody out there? Antecedents of trust in global virtual teams. *Journal of Management Information Systems 14(4);* Jarvenpaa, S.L. & Leidner, D.E. (1998). Communication and trust in global virtual teams. *Journal of Computer-Mediate Communication, 3(4)*

[107] Werry, C.C. (1996) cited in Wallace, P. (1999). *The Psychology of the Internet*, Cambridge, Cambridge University Press.

[108] Zimmerman, D. & West, C. (1975). Sex roles, interruptions, and silences in conversation. In B. Thorme & N Henley. (Eds.), *Language and Sex: Difference and dominance (pp105-129).* Rowley, MA. Newbury House. Cited in Wallace, P. (1999). *The Psychology of the Internet*, Cambridge, Cambridge University Press. p114.

Say you're in the middle of an online chat with someone and then you suddenly stop to make a cup of coffee, answer the phone or answer a colleague's urgent query. The other person will have to second-guess the reason for your non-response – they may think they've said something to upset you, that you're not interested in continuing the conversation, that you're just plain rude or a host of other things. Leaving them hanging in this way can be problematic when it comes to developing trust in the relationship. So it's worth making an extra effort when chatting online with people you don't know that well to provide extra 'signposts' which tell them what to expect – a simple 'got to go back to work now, catch you later' is fine. People cannot mindread, so you have to be even more polite, well-mannered and thoughtful than you are face-to-face.

Online business networks like LinkedIn couldn't operate effectively without trust either, although they develop it in different ways. LinkedIn's New User Starter Guide[109] states 'Ensure your connections represent your 'real-world' network.' In other words, your LinkedIn network should be a mirror image of your real-life network, and you only connect with people that you have already worked with and would be willing to recommend. These are the connections that you know and trust. Ask yourself, would I be prepared to recommend all of the people in my business network?

Ecademy, on the other hand, operates on a slightly different model. Trust is still at the heart of Ecademy online relationship, but here you're encouraged to connect with as many people as you can as quickly as you can, then to develop a good relationship with them (online and face-to-face), building trust that way. To quote Ecademy:

To build a strong business relationship, you must first gain trust from one another through having a personal relationship, this is critical before you can expect to move onto a relationship where a transaction or a referral can take place:

Relationships > Trust > Trade

[109] http://learn.linkedin.com/new-users/

Perhaps because Ecademy promotes online connection with people you don't actually know and haven't met yet, it has published a code of ethics and values to help guide members' activities on the website and manage their expectations. There is no need for LinkedIn to do this, since all members ostensibly already know everyone in their network.

Ecademy Code[110]:

1. *Members should be polite and courteous in their written tone. Sadly, without the face-to-face advantages of our offline events, body language cannot be read and therefore sarcasm and innuendo can be misinterpreted and cause offence.*

2. *Honesty is critical and we will not tolerate misrepresentation of names and services. Don't be afraid to reveal the real you as well as the business you; people like to do business with people.*

3. *Kindness towards your fellow member is encouraged. Being willing to help, listen, advise and pass referrals is a core principle at Ecademy. Help one another by giving not taking and never ask for something in return.*

4. *Being open-minded to the opinions of others will help you get more from Ecademy. Many opinions are shared here. Being over-sensitive or closed-minded will restrict your opportunity to learn. Remember, constructive criticism can be very valuable.*

5. *Giving personal criticism or airing your views against a member must be directed carefully as a message direct to them. Public attacks on individuals are noted by members and the management team. If they occur regularly from the same individual, warnings will be issued to the offending member with the appropriate explanation of the way their behaviour has offended.*

[110] http://www.ecademy.com/node.php?id=31751

6. *Treat others as you would like to be treated, a great saying, and so true here. Act with professional maturity if you join debates and always keep focused on the topic of the debate that you are joining. They are great fun when treated with humour and courtesy.*
7. *Thank and acknowledge members who deserve it. If someone has been kind then add this to their testimonial area.*
8. *Welcome members from around the world into your network. They can provide you with help on business issues, cultural questions, travel, holidays, the best restaurant to visit on their city and even retrieve a teddy left on holiday (it has been known!).*

To assist in building personal relationships between its members, Ecademy also offers organised speed networking events, workshops and presentations on a variety of business-related subjects where you can get to meet your online contacts face-to-face. To find a networking event to attend, simply click on the 'Events' tab in Ecademy to browse by date or location. Many are free, or at a nominal cost. Some are run in partnership with other well-established business networks such as NRG[111] and BNI[112]. If you're keen to get the most out of your Ecademy network, these face-to-face events are essential.

It's worth remembering that if you stick to the principle of connecting only to people you know well enough to recommend, your LinkedIn business network is likely to grow much more slowly than your Facebook or Ecademy network. So you have a choice to make. There's nothing really stopping you trying to create a much wider network on LinkedIn by inviting people you don't know well enough to recommend (or don't know at all) to join your network, although you may receive a few rejections or get asked to provide an endorsement for them. As a result, we draw you back to your networking goal(s). Randomly adding people to your network is

[111] http://www.nrg-networks.com/
[112] http://www.bni-europe.com/

unlikely to generate much benefit for you. And the reverse is also true. Just because you know someone doesn't mean that you have to connect to them in a public space!

When you do invite someone to join you on LinkedIn, you're asked to specify how you know them – you can select from the following options:

- Colleague – you have to state which company
- Classmate – state which school
- As business partners – state which company
- As a friend
- Through a group or association – state which one
- Other – in which case you have to state their email address.

If you select the option 'I don't know this contact', your invitation won't be sent.

As we suggested in Chapter 1, it's a good idea to include a personalised invitation, rather than just send the standard LinkedIn text.

Connecting in Ecademy is much more straightforward. Simply find the person you want to invite using the search function. In the box write a short personal invitation and click the 'Send Contact Request' button.

Top Tip

In Ecademy you don't have to be in someone's network already to be able to view their profile, the clubs they belong to or their network connections. And because most Ecademists are keen to make as many connections as possible, they will still welcome an approach from someone they don't know, providing you make the request personally, adding a reason why they might want to connect with you. Make sure you read their profile before getting in touch, in case they have given any pointers to their preferred method of contact.

The previous chapter took you through the ins and outs of setting up an online profile in a selection of social networking sites. Now we'll focus on what you can do next to make the most of your online presence.

The benefits of joining professional groups and clubs online

Joining a group or club on a social networking site, be it business or social, is a great way to connect to people who share the same interests or passions as you. There are literally hundreds of thousands of different groups, representing every kind of industry, trade, opinion, hobby and special interest, as well as those specifically related to corporations, not-for-profit organisations and university and college alumni groups. Joining a group allows you to discuss current hot-topic issues with like-minded individuals. Of course, the groups and clubs you find on LinkedIn and Ecademy are largely related to business, professional or industry subjects, although you can also find a large number of support or personal interest groups such as The Dyslexia Advantage club. Groups on Facebook and other non-business networking sites tend to be much more wide-ranging, esoteric or just plain daft, and include such clubs as 'Dental floss makes me nervous' , 'I have worked in retail, and thus have lost all faith in humanity' and 'I love it when bus drivers wave to each other'. Some social networking groups have serious objectives, such as campaigning for political and social change, or they may have none at all.

The purpose of joining groups and clubs on social networking sites is threefold:

- To find out what other individuals in your professional field are doing. You can discover a wealth of information about your actual and potential competitors this way.
- To publicise your name and your professional expertise.
- To discover other information that might help you make more contacts, find more opportunities or grow your business.

How to join a group on LinkedIn

Unless you know which group or club you are looking for, your search may return pages of results, in which case you simply have to trawl through them all until you find the one you are looking for. Remember that the membership of some LinkedIn groups is determined by the group's manager. So until they have approved you, your membership is 'pending', and you cannot start new discussion threads or respond to existing ones. Other groups allow anyone to join.

- Go to your home page and click on 'Groups' on the left navigation bar.
- Click on the 'Groups Directory' tab on the right hand side.
- Using the 'Search Groups' box, type in the name of the group you are looking for or a keyword and/or choose a 'Category' from the drop down menu. This will help to narrow your search.
- Click on 'Search'.
- Once you have found a group you want to join, click on the title of the group to reach its homepage. Assuming you agree with it aims and objectives, click the yellow 'join group' button.
- You then get a 'join group' page where you have several options, for example to display the group logo on your profile page. Make any necessary changes, then click the blue 'join group' button.
- If the group isn't managed by an administrator, you can start posting new threads and/or starting new discussions straight away. If the group membership is managed, you will need to wait until your membership is approved first.

How to join a group on Facebook

Finding the right group to join in Facebook should not be underestimated. For example, there are over 500 psychology groups. They're listed in order of number of members, with the largest first. Of course this means that those with the highest number continue to grow, whereas those which appear after about page 5 of your search are unlikely to be found, unless you're persistent, or you already know what you're looking for.

- Click on 'applications' at the bottom left hand side of any Facebook page.
- You will then see a list of the groups recently joined by your Facebook friends on the left hand side, and any groups that you have joined on the right.
- To find other groups to join, either type in the name of the group you're looking for in the search field, or use the 'browse groups' tab on the top left of the page. You can then filter the groups using the 'network' and 'type' drop-down menus. Types are then divided into subtypes. So if you select 'business' as your group type, you will find subtypes to choose from, e.g. companies, home business, PR and marketing.
- You can join any open group. Click on the group title to find more information about the group and check it is the one you want to join. Most groups have some information about their aims and objectives on the group homepage. Assuming you're happy with these, click on the 'join group' button.
- Some groups are 'closed', which means that you must be invited or approved by the group administrator. In this case, click on the 'request to join' button, and wait until your membership is approved.

How to join an Ecademy club

- Find the club you're interested in from the search facility (this is probably the hardest part – there are so many to choose from).
- Some Ecademy clubs are 'private' which means they are by invitation only. You can apply to join, although you may not be successful. Until you are a member, you can't browse the club's forum or its membership list.
- Other clubs are open to anyone and everyone, and you can look at the content of the forum and the membership list without being a member.
- Read the introductory information to check what the club is for and its terms of membership.
- If you want to go ahead, click the small blue 'join' button on the right hand side of the page.
- You will then be reminded of general terms and conditions of Ecademy clubs. Assuming you are still happy, click the grey 'join' button.

Posting a new message in an Ecademy club is easy:

- Click 'Forum'
- Click 'New Thread'
- Type in your message
- Click 'Preview Thread'
- Click 'Post Thread'.

It's as well to be aware that you can delete messages you've posted in Ecademy clubs and in LinkedIn groups if you later change your mind. You just need to find your message, click the 'edit' button and click on 'delete message'.

Top tip – if you're not sure which groups or clubs will be useful, have a look at those your connections belong to.

Once you've joined the group or club, it's worth spending some time reading through the discussions and the posts that other members have made. This will help you get a feel for topics that are current, those which have already been discussed and put to one side, as well as to understand the way that participants respond. Whilst it's possible to make some general suggestions about what to do once you've joined an online networking group or club, they do develop their own particular norms over time and what is acceptable in one group may be frowned upon in another.

Getting to know your LinkedIn Group:

1. Click on your new group's link located on the left hand side of your home page.
2. Click on the 'Overview' page – this displays the topics which are currently being discussed in the group as well as News and Updates, such as who has joined the group in the past week and who has commented on which discussion threads. You can also see the News and Updates by clicking on the separate tabs.
3. Explore the 'Members' tab. Holding your cursor over their name for a few seconds returns a mini profile, from where you can access their full profile or send a message. So you can find out about their background, expertise, achievements and interests, all of which may be very relevant to you.

Getting to know your Ecademy Club:

1. Click on the 'clubs' tab from your profile page and select the club that you want to browse
2. From the left-hand navigation menu, click 'Forum'. From here you can browse all the discussion threads. Once you have found one that interests you, click on the title to reveal all the threads related to this topic.
3. You can also use the left hand navigation menu to search the forum or find the last message posted.
4. Explore the list of members – by alphabetical order of first name, or by photo, which shows the photos of those members recently online. You can click on each photo to access the member's profile.

So using groups and clubs is one way to find and connect to other network users who have similar experience and interests, and to provide mutual assistance with business issues or questions. It is also an essential way to make new connections, to publicise your name and start building your reputation in a particular field of professional knowledge, skill or expertise.

Google groups

Google groups are a great idea in theory. They allow you to discuss issues and topics that you're interested in and knowledgeable about. Once you're a member of the group, you can reply to a message that someone else has posted, or post a message or question of your own. The difficulty arises in trying to find a suitable group, although Google search criteria are more thorough than LinkedIn's, and allow you to sort the groups by size of membership (although quantity is not always an indicator of quality) as well as see when they were last posted to. Some groups are moderated, and membership is by approval. You may be asked to explain your credentials by the group owner, to ensure that you are a bona fide professional. Some groups are open access, which means that anyone can join. Where this is the case, you can't be sure that everyone who joins is also a professional, or shares your interests. If you look at some of the discussion threads for some groups, for example, they appear to be direct postings about products or services, which are more self-interest than an attempt to provide value for other readers. In practice it can be quite a task to weed out the wheat from the chaff of Google groups. So you need to think about how much time you're going to invest in finding a suitable group to join.

Note that you can set up your own Google group if you can't find one that matches your interests and expertise. Providing you plan in advance how you are going to publicise your Group (for example, emailing details to your friends and acquaintances), and make a regular commitment to update the content, this is a great way to publicise yourself. If you can reuse material that you already post on a blog, so much the better.

When you set up a group you have three levels of access to choose from:

- **Public** – Anyone can read the archives. Anyone can join, but only members can post messages, view the members list, create pages and upload files.

- **Announcement only.** This means that anyone can read the archives, and anyone can join but only group managers can post messages, view the members list, create pages and upload files.

- **Restricted access.** These are groups where membership must be approved. Many of the professional, corporate and academic Google groups have restricted access which ensures that only bona fide members can join. Only members can post messages, read the archives, view the members list, create pages and upload files. But do note that your group and its archives do not appear in public Google search results or the directory.

Joining online groups

Moderation/administration

Some online groups and clubs, especially email distribution lists (sometimes called 'listservs' after the technology on which they are based) are moderated; in some groups, all posts are approved before they are published; in others, the moderator may edit or delete messages if they are considered unsuitable in some way. A moderated list or group thus puts the moderator in the equivalent position as a newspaper editor.

LinkedIn groups are administrated by the group owner. He or she approves your membership of the group, and can throw you out if you post inappropriate messages. Some groups, like the CIPD group on LinkedIn discourage direct selling; others are more relaxed about it – Ecademy has a 'Marketplace' function specifically for you to advertise your goods and services, as well as many clubs which encourage direct selling and marketing.

Some of the groups have 'rules of engagement', which will help guide you in what you can and cannot post. For instance, Mike Morrison, Director of RapidBI Ltd and administrator of the CIPD LinkedIn group, has published the following 'Conduct Guidelines' to ensure that the group discussion and interaction remains relevant and beneficial to all members:

1. *We welcome debate and dissent.*
2. *Please respect other people's views and beliefs and consider their impact when making your contribution.*
3. *We will remove any content that may put us in legal jeopardy.*
4. *Keep comments relevant.*
5. *We reserve the right to remove any posts that are obviously commercial or otherwise spam-like.*
6. *The platform is ours, but the conversation belongs to everybody.*
7. *We are here to network providing value and not to 'collect' contacts.*

Don't get put off by the fact that some groups prohibit or discourage overt selling; this can be a blessing in disguise. For a start the group discussion space isn't littered with irritating adverts for products and services which you don't want. Secondly, it means that you really do have to focus on honing your marketing skills, by providing well-presented materials that other group members will find interesting and engaging. Referring to your knowledge or experience is fine, as is linking to whitepapers or blog posts on the subject, as long as what you say is useful to other participants and relevant to the discussion in hand, or linked to a current hot topic. Note that when you have posted your comment to the discussion in a LinkedIn group, you have 15 minutes in which to edit it.

Ecademy groups have overt terms and conditions[113], such as:

- *Do not sell or advertise goods or services unless the club is specifically stated to be for 'Business'.*
- *Do not headhunt or solicit members for career moves.*
- *Do not 'Spam' or send repeated messages.*
- *Do not insult other members by using racial or sexual remarks.*
- *Do not give out any personal information.*
- *Do not give out any personal information about anyone else.*
- *Groups cannot be formed as a disguise or front to Ecademy member recruitment into MLM*[114] *or Network Marketing products and services.*
- *Ecademy is not a network marketing or MLM company and will not accept this kind of activity within its trusted business network environment.*
- *Ecademy reserve the right to rename a group or delete inappropriate groups without notice.*
- *Ecademy own all membership data, all text is copyright © of the author and The Ecademy Ltd. Logos are copyright © their respective owners. The use of the Ecademy brand (name or*

[113] http://www.ecademy.com/node.php?id=109458

[114] Mutli-Level Marketing

logo) is prohibited without prior permission from Ecademy, with the exception of regional Networking Groups (i.e. Ecademy London, Milan Ecademy, etc.).

Introducing yourself

Introductions are necessary when joining some forms of internet-based discussion groups, such as academic and professional listservs. (A listserv is an automatic mailing list; when an email is addressed to the mailing list it is automatically sent to everyone on the list. This is very similar to what happens in an internet forum or news group, except that the emails are only available to those people who subscribe to the list). Some listservs are open to anyone who has an interest in the subject, whereas others are by invitation only. See the section below on how to write an effective personal introduction. Note that it isn't necessary to introduce yourself in a LinkedIn, Ecademy or Facebook group. Your name, photo and/or professional headline will appear next to your comment, and anyone who is interested in finding out more about you can click on these to view your detailed profile.

How to write an effective personal introduction:

Unlike social networking sites, listservs do not have profiles, so when you join, other participants need to know a bit about you and what your interest is in the group. This is the time to refer back to your 'Elevator Pitch' (see Chapter 2). Obviously we're assuming here that your interest in the topic of the listserv is genuine and that you are not going to join it merely to promote yourself and tout for business! In all likelihood this will be against the group rules anyway (see 'rules of engagement', below), and your membership would be quickly suspended by the moderator.

Before you introduce yourself, see if there are any overt participation guidelines or a code of conduct that you need to be aware of first. Then, search the listserv for other introductions to see how other people have introduced themselves; you may pick up some good tips, or notice things to avoid. Some listserv members 'lurk' on the listserv for months or years without ever contributing, but if you want and expect to participate in the discussion, it's good etiquette to have introduced yourself first.

We've seen some personal introductions which cover at least two sides of A4 in size 10 font. Other members are unlikely to read something as long as this. As with all online communication, make your introduction easy on the eye by structuring what you write into bullet points. Keep your sentences short and use the spellchecker. The rules about how to write effective emails apply here. But even if you've toiled for hours to hone your personal introduction into an absolute masterpiece, you shouldn't necessarily expect to get an acknowledgement from anyone else on the listserv.

Top tips on writing a good online introduction

Use an appropriate subject header.

Be friendly, using a greeting and a sign-off.

Structure what you write, using bullet points if necessary.

Keep your sentences short

Use the spellchecker.

Use professional language.

Provide an outline of your career history if relevant.

Summarise your professional interests in the listserv.

Depending on the listserv's code of conduct, include your company name and/or link to your company website in your sign-off.

Following some simple rules will ensure that your first foray into the world of listservs will be a positive experience, and that you will establish your credibility from the start.

Personal Introduction: example

Hello

My name is Christopher Jones. I'm an independent chartered occupational psychologist (Masters in Occupational Psychology) working with organisations in the applied positive psychology and coaching fields.

Professional interests: creating communities in organisations to improve employee engagement and job satisfaction.

Recently I have researched the use of new technologies, especially social networking.

My MSc research focused on the well-being of professional people.

I look forward to participating in the listserv discussion to find out more about these subjects and explore others.

Best wishes

Christopher

ABC123 Psychologists
www.abc123-psychologists.com

Video introductions

Whilst most social networking sites rely on communicating via the written word (more about that later), some like Ecademy and Twitter now allow you to upload video clips, which could be used to introduce yourself, and to summarise your experience and what you can offer. For instance, you could record a short clip of yourself and upload it to Twitter using the Bubbletweet application[115]. Why not

[115] www.bubbletweet.com

practise your 'elevator pitch' and use this as your own personal advertisement?

When you are using video, you have to think about both what you are going to say and how you say this. So where the video clip is recorded, what you wear and how you speak will all be part of the communication. Put as much thought into these parts as into the script which you plan to deliver.

It's also worth remembering that visual attention is short, to make your video clip short and snappy, maybe 20-40 seconds in length. If you do go for a 40 second clip, ensure that it's more than a single camera shot with a talking head. Film the same clip from different angles and edit this together, so the clip holds the listener's full attention.

Understanding the 'rules of engagement'

We always advise that you skim-read as much of the previous group, club or listserv discussion as you can, in order to get a sense of the kind of topics included, what participants are interested in, and the way topics get discussed. Otherwise you might find yourself in the awkward situation of repeating something that has already been mentioned or that people already know, going off-topic, or worse, finding that you have misunderstood the purpose of the listserv completely, and have the embarrassment of a public reproach, as this example from the soc.singles Usenet group shows[116]:

> **Newbie:** *Hi, I'm a 23 year old graduate student and would like to communicate with any females on this news net. (posted for a non-net friend).*

[116] Smith,C.B., McLaughlin, M.L., and Osborne, K.K. (1997). Conduct control on Usenet. Journal of Computer-Mediated Communication, 2 (4), (http://jcmc.indiana.edu/vol2/issue4/smith.html) cited in Wallace, P. (2001). The psychology of the internet. Cambridge,UK. Cambridge University Press, pp122-123

Old hat: *Well, howdy! Finally a request for a female that doesn't specify species – you wouldn't believe how many people on this net want a woman, which of course means a person. *giggle*.*

*My name is Susa, and I'm a five-year-old Lemur in the Philly Zoo. My measurements are 12-12-12, which is considered quite sexy for a Lemur. *giggle* My hobbies include running around, climbing trees, and picking lice. I hope you have a nice thick head of hair!*

*I only write to stupid people who post personals on a soc.singles; the other ones are too smart for me – we lemurs may be very_cuddly *giggle* but we tend to be on the low end of the smarts scale. I know that with that post, you'll be really dumb for a human, and perfect for me! *giggle*'*

Recipients of the public reproach frequently never reply, although this one did:

Newbie: *In reference to my posting a few hours ago...I have just discovered that this is the wrong news group! Thanks to so many people, among others, so if you'll all quit sending me messages I move on.*

OK? But those of you who seem to have nothing better to do, feel free to do whatever you want!

The value of asking questions

Membership of groups or clubs in Facebook, LinkedIn or Ecademy can be used to enhance your professional image and reputation directly and indirectly. For instance, you can uncover a wealth of new information about your industry or field of expertise, as well as get work done, by asking new questions. You can ask for direct help or advice with a business issue – the CIPD members' forum is bursting with queries about practical implications of employment law for example. Members of the Open University Business School alumni group in LinkedIn regularly ask for advice on everything from new marketing strategies to help with completing trademark applications. You will find that, providing your question is appropriate to the remit of the group or club (see Rules of Engagement, above), most members are very willing to help. So you can find out all sorts of useful information, as well as make some great new connections, by asking well-timed, intelligent questions (or providing answers to another member's question). As mentioned above, make sure you search the group for existing threads on the topic before you ask your question, or you may get an unexpectedly curt response when you discover that it has been asked and answered many times in the past.

Of course, networking is all about give and take, and you need to make sure that you share your knowledge and expertise with the group as well. Doing this is a great way to enhance your reputation. But as well as posting questions to your group, LinkedIn has a great 'Answer' function which allows members with more than 5 connections to post up to 10 business-related questions each month to the wider LinkedIn network. In other words, you don't have to be a group member to be able to post your own questions, answer other members' questions yourself, or read their answers. This is an especially useful facility for the growing number of freelancers and independent consultants who mostly work on their own – LinkedIn Answers acts as an office full of virtual colleagues who have a huge range of expertise to share. Note that LinkedIn warns against asking questions just to connect to those people who reply.

The LinkedIn Answer function can also be used to ask for specific business information or advice. If you use questions to recruit, advertise, or publicise the fact that you're looking for a job, however, you must tick the relevant checkboxes when you create the question, or risk having it flagged as inappropriate.

How to ask a good question using LinkedIn's Answers

Key rule 1: Make your question short and to the point. Up to 2000 characters are available, but you should really only use a fraction of that number.

As with all written communication, we think that clarity is fundamental, so make sure your question is clearly stated as a question, and that it's easy to understand. 'Can you recommend any good books on organisational change management?' is a well-stated question, whereas 'Good books on change management' suggests that you're providing a list for others to comment on.

Key rule 2: in the body of the posting, provide some context to the question.

In other words, provide just enough background information to ensure that the reader understands what you're asking. You have up to 4000 characters, but we recommend that you keep your text succinct. You can always add a clarification later if needs be.

As for appropriate subject matters for questions, LinkedIn advises against asking directly for introductions to other contacts, suggesting that other members may flag such questions as inappropriate, which could result in you being blocked from asking questions completely.

Points mean prizes: earning expertise through LinkedIn Answers

Of course, it will have occurred to you that there is another side to the use of questions. By providing a prompt, helpful and courteous response, you can demonstrate your knowledge and expertise in your professional field. If you look at the bottom of the LinkedIn Answers homepage for example, you can see a list of this week's top experts, i.e. those people who have proven their expertise by answering questions. Judging from the volume of answers that some people make in a week, some people clearly spend all their spare time on LinkedIn, and are making this a profession in its own right. You can earn a point every time the questioner picks your answer as the best one, and the more points you earn, the higher up the rankings of experts you will appear.

How to become recognised as an expert on LinkedIn

LinkedIn experts are the people whose opinions and know-how is respected; the 'star' award helps raise your profile. Writing answers is a great way to demonstrate your writing ability as well as your subject knowledge to those members who read your answer and review your profile.

Find relevant questions in those subjects you know about.

Answer those questions in an engaging, persuasive and interesting way.

You earn a point every time your response is selected as the best answer by the member who asked the question.

But remember that answering questions privately will not earn any points towards gaining expert status.

Advanced Search

Twitter recommendations: how to use #FollowFriday

At this point it's appropriate to bring in Twitter again. As we mentioned in Chapter 2, many people think that Twitter is only about keeping friends and colleagues up to date with details of your latest escapades. Indeed, many Twitter users do just this, which is fine if that's all you want to do. But there is a whole other side to Twitter which probably surprises even its inventors, and that is its development into a fantastic marketing medium. Take the '#FollowFriday' phenomenon, for instance. #FollowFriday, invented by Micah Baldwin[117], is a way of acknowledging the Twitter users who you value in some way. Perhaps they have helped you out, given you information, or you respect their opinions and expertise. By giving someone a #FollowFriday (which you only do on a Friday, of course!) it means that you recommend other people to follow them. (See Chapter 2 for more information about following people on Twitter.) By endorsing them in this way, other Twitter users can easily see who is worth following. So by helping others and by posting valuable content and links, albeit it using only 140 characters, you can receive a #FollowFriday recommendation, your reputation can be enhanced, and you can hope to acquire more followers as a result.

Top tip

Take care when making #FollowFriday endorsements. Recommending people just because they're friends or family can backfire on you if their tweets turn out to be irrelevant, tasteless or just plain dull.

How to avoid online aggression

The final section of this chapter looks at the phenomenon of 'flaming', the online equivalent of road-rage. It's worth being aware that sometimes simple mistakes (such as the one mentioned on page 98 above) can escalate into a full-scale flame war, i.e. the trading of aggressive, antagonistic and overtly hostile comments between two or more members. Flaming can include:

- Swearing
- Impolite statements
- Explicit sexual language

[117] http://mashable.com/2009/03/06/twitter-followfriday/

- Name-calling
- Expressions of negative emotion
- Use of exclamation marks
- Use of capital letters (the online equivalent of shouting)
- Use of sarcasm.

Research shows that inappropriate or aggressive behaviour is significantly more common in online email discussions than in those held via video-conference or face to face[118]. There are a number of reasons for this. Firstly, because discussions are text-based, the recipient of the message has time to reflect on the content of the message and prepare a counter-argument (which can then escalate). It is also relatively easy to 'dissect' the comments made by others, quote them out of context or prepare a point-by-point counter-argument, whereas this is not so easy to do in a face-to-face discussion. It has also been suggested that in text-based exchanges the recipient doesn't need to remember the details of the message, as they would have to in face-to-face discussion, so they can focus much more on developing and honing their own counter-argument. The emotions aroused on reading a text-based message can be experienced repeatedly as the message is read and re-read.

Other factors contributing to aggressive behaviour include:

- **Anonymity** – it has been suggested that anonymity, or the illusion of it, is one of the key components of online aggression, the reason being that people are less socially inhibited when they think that their behaviour or comments can't be easily attributed to them. In one of the early studies into communication via computer, it was found that anonymous groups made more than six times as many

[118] Castella,V.O., Abad, A.M.Z, Alonso, F.P. & Silla, J.M.P. (2000). The influence of familiarity among group members, group atmosphere and assertiveness on uninhibited behaviour through three different communication media. *Computers in Human Behaviour, 16,* 141-59; Sproull & Kiesler (1986).Reducing social context clues: electronic mail ion organizational communication. *Management Science, 32,* 1492-512.

uninhibited comments are did the groups who were not anonymous.[119]

Remaining anonymous (relatively or absolutely), at the same time as being able to make contact publicly, is one feature of the online world which increases the likelihood of aggressive behaviour[120]. Before the advent of the internet, the worst that could happen would be a poison-pen letter, or an anonymous letter to the press. Of course, in social networking sites like LinkedIn you're not really anonymous, but listservs and Google groups are slightly different: there's relatively little deterrent. For many transgressors, the worst that can happen is that they get banned from the group, in which case they could easily re-invent themselves with a new hotmail email address.

- The **send button** – certain features, like the send button, make rash or impulsive replies (and occasionally aggressive or otherwise provocative replies) more likely. How often have you fired off a hasty email in the emotional heat of the moment, only to regret it later?

So a word of warning: you should be prepared for the possibility that sometimes the response you get to your posting, however innocuous or innocent it was, may be disproportionately negative. Of course, as reasonable professionals, in the cool light of day we would never believe that we could get caught up in a flame war, yet there are several features of the internet which make aggression from ordinarily well-behaved people more common online than you might think. So even if you're usually pretty mild-mannered and easy-going, just be aware that on the internet you can behave in an

[119] Siegel, J. Dubrovsky, V., Kiesler, S., & McGuire, T. (1983). Group processes in computer-mediated communications. Study cited in Kielser, S., Siegel, J. & McGuire, T.W. (1984). Social psychological aspects of computer-mediated communication. *American psychologist, 39(10),* 1123-1134.

[120] Rubin, A.M (1994). Media uses and effects: a uses-and-gratifications perspective. In J. Bryant & D. Zillmann (Eds.), *Media effects: advances in theory and research. LEA's communication series* (pp.417-36). Hillsdale:Erlbaum.

out-of-character way.

You might think that flaming can't happen in social networking sites, but it does. Fortunately, sites like LinkedIn and Ecademy are better controlled than other online meeting places so outright aggression is likely to be flagged and dealt with quickly.

4

How to create and manage your brand

Reputation

> *'Whenever men are discussed (and especially princes, who are more exposed to view), they are noted for various qualities which earn them either praise or condemnation. Some for example are held to be generous and others miserly. Some are held to be benefactors, others are called grasping; some cruel, others compassionate; one man faithless, another faithful, one man weak and cowardly, another fierce and courageous....A prince need not necessarily have all the good qualities I mentioned above, but he should certainly appear to have them'.*
>
> *Machiavelli, The Prince.*

When it comes to reputation, it seems that perception is more important than reality. Indeed it could be said that those who make it to the top of organisations are typically the ones who have the political skill necessary to promote themselves and their achievements effectively, regardless of the reality. In this chapter we'll focus on the importance of creating a persuasive and effective impression on the internet and what you can to do to maintain your reputation as well as to what to do if things start going a little pear-shaped. Of the books written on the subject of 'personal branding', very few specifically address the question from an online perspective, even though more and more business communication is carried out over the internet. But it's important that you appreciate the similarities and differences between the methods of creating face-to-face and online impressions if you're going to get the most out of your online networking.

From a psychological perspective, impression formation and impression management are two separate processes. Impression management (or self-presentation) is all about the activities that you engage in, in order to project the most favourable image possible. This might happen when you're in a job interview and you want to convince the HR director that you're the most competent candidate and the most committed to the organisation, or when you're out on a date, and you want the man or woman you're meeting to think you're the kindest, most generous and witty person they've met. Impression formation refers to how they, the HR Director or the person you're dating, create a mental image of you, based on their knowledge and beliefs about you and on your appearance and behaviour, both verbal and non-verbal. And yes you can, of course, influence the impression you give others and the way they receive it by the types of things you do or don't do.

Can you judge a book by its cover?

Well sadly for those of us who are no more than averagely attractive, people make judgements based on physical appearance and observed behaviours all the time: it's said that recruiters generally make their minds up about interview candidates within the first three minutes of meeting them. You might therefore think that appearance and behaviour is less important for computer-mediated interactions like email – after all, unless you're on a webcam 24/7, no-one can see what you get up to anyway. One of us once interviewed one of the UK's leading life coaches, who very openly claimed that the best thing about working from home was that she didn't have to get changed out of her pyjamas before she rang her clients. Of course, if you're a little bit of an exhibitionist with a penchant for feather boas or exotic undergarments and you have a tendency to post photos of yourself in various states of undress on your Facebook profile, we do advise that you think twice about the impression you're giving, and at least make sure that you're using the privacy filters and are careful who you let become friends: for more on this subject see Chapter 2.

But are there other, more subtle ways, that you give off clues about yourself, just by the way you write emails, for instance? Well, you'll not be surprised to know that the answer is a definite yes! But we'll leave until later the dark and murky world of 'leakage' (a lovely term, which we hasten to add refers to the transference of meaning in non-verbal communication). First of all, we really do need to explore the whole question of identity in more depth.

Can you see the real me?

(The Who, 1974[121])

When we stop to think about what 'identity' actually is, from psychological and sociological perspectives, we can see straightaway that it's much more complex than merely a collection of facts about you, such as your name, age, gender and job; it has multiple and dynamic dimensions. Sociologists have defined identity as 'a sense of self that develops as the child differentiates from parents and family and takes a place in society'[122], so one's identity is at the same time something which makes us different, and something which is shaped through our membership of social groups and helps us integrate with them[123]. As far back as the 1950s it was suggested that identity is socially constructed, and could be better understood as a series of theatrical performances, where we try to portray ourselves in a particular light depending on the situation we're in and the people we're with[124]. One way of looking at this is to say that everyone has the opportunity to present and represent themselves in different ways (e.g. how you dress, what

[121] http://www.youtube.com/watch?v=o9Or4QGI80Y

[122] Jary, D. & Jary, J. (1991). *Collins dictionary of sociology*. London. HarperCollins.

[123] Jenkins, R. (1996). *Social identity*. London. Routledge.

[124] Goffman, E. (1959). The presentation of self in everyday life. Garden City, NY: Anchor/Doubleday.

you say, how you behave and so on), and learning to do this effectively is a part of growing up. We all do it, all the time, whether consciously or subconsciously, to a greater or lesser extent.

At the moment, the internet, in particular 3D virtual worlds like Second Life, can provide almost endless opportunities to try out new identities and new ways of behaving; as the saying goes, 'on the internet, no one knows you're a dog'[125]. It is perfectly possible to join an internet chat room pretending to be a different age and gender; other users would be none the wiser (see below, and also Chapter 1, for further information about false identities). It has been suggested that playing with different identities helps to bring about psychological maturity[126], but problems arise on the internet when the boundaries between role-playing and real life become blurred. Identity swapping can easily tip over into deceit. So if you're contemplating 'radical identity surgery', you do need to watch out for this; other users may not take kindly to being misled, whatever your intentions. It's too soon to say whether recent internet developments, such as Spark.ly[127] (a meta tool which enables users to consolidate their social presence from across various social networking sites, manage their connections in groups, and write once and be read by all or selected portions of their network) will encourage or discourage users from maintaining multiple online identities.

Now that we've talked a little about online identity, and the possibility (and some of the dangers) of developing multiple personalities, let's turn to the thorny question of impression management.

Are you a leopard or a chameleon?

Now there will probably be a certain proportion of you who believe

[125] Cartoon by Peter Steiner in the New Yorker, 5th July 1993. http://www.unc.edu/depts/jomc/academics/dri/idog.html

[126] Turkle, S. (1995). *Life on the screen: identity in the age of the internet.* New York. Simon and Schuster.

[127] http://www.free-press-release.com/news/200906/1244773861.html

that impression management, self-presentation, or self-promotion is at best a slightly unsavoury activity, or at worst, downright dishonest, manipulative and unethical. You might prefer to live according to the software slogan 'What You See Is What You Get'; images of slippery spin-doctors from political world spring to mind with astonishing ease. You may, as a result, feel pretty uncomfortable about entering into a world where you not only need to promote yourself, but you also need to do so in a very public way. Don't worry, we can understand this; there is a psychological term for this too!

It's called 'self-monitoring'[128]. Basically, people who are high self-monitors are much more comfortable with adapting what they say and do to suit the situation they find themselves in. They're a bit like chameleons. They're likely to agree with statements such as 'in different situations and with different people, I often act like a very different person', or 'I would make a very good actor', or 'I'm not always the person I appear to be'. On the plus side, people who are high self-monitors are better at picking up and adapting to the subtle clues from others such as their facial expressions, and other non-verbal communication and they're better at using their voices to convey particular nuances of meaning. But if they're at the extreme, that is, very high self-monitors, they can be seen as inconsistent and perhaps even a bit opportunist.

On the other hand there are people who are low self monitors – the leopards who don't change their spots. These people are 'themselves' regardless of the situation they're in. They're likely to agree with statements such as 'I wouldn't change my opinions, or the way I do things, in order to please someone else or win their favour', 'I can only argue for ideas that I already believe' and 'I have never been good at games like charades or improvisational acting'. On the plus side, low self-monitors can be seen to be very solid and reliable. In the extreme, however, they can be seen to be

---

[128] Snyder, M., & Gangestad, S. (1986). On the nature of self-monitoring: Matters of assessment, matters of validity. *Journal of Personality and Social Psychology*, *51*(1), 125-139. Snyder, M (1987). Public appearances, private realities: The psychology of self-monitoring. New York: Freeman.

insensitive, uncompromising and inflexible. One of us has worked with such a person who was constantly running into conflicts with other people and had no idea why this was happening; they thought they were being true to themselves. As with most things in life, finding a balance between the two is often the most effective position to take.

You'll probably know instinctively whether you're a low or a high self-monitor. Either way, it's worth reflecting on how this affects what you do to present yourself most positively, and what the pros and cons are of your individual approach. High self-monitors won't have a problem with promoting themselves, whereas low self-monitors may feel more uncomfortable. For these 'leopards' then, we would give the following advice.

Firstly, even WYSIWYG software is not what it seems! Under the surface there is a huge amount of activity going on to ensure that what you see is indeed what you get.

Secondly, as we discussed in Chapter 3 in the section on comfort zones, doing things which you don't think are 'you' can be a bit daunting at first, especially if you're an introvert. We suggest that you start small and take it one small step at a time.

Thirdly, there is a perspective that we may as well consciously try to take control of the impression we make, since all of us do it unconsciously anyway.

'[H]uman beings cannot not communicate [and] the few situations in life in which human beings fail to impression manage are thought to be rare exceptions.'[129]

In other words, impression management and positive self-promotion are presumed to be dynamic, ongoing, and inevitable human behaviour. Whether you like it or not!

Anonymity versus visibility

Before we get into the practicalities of managing your impression

[129] Sallot, L. (2002). What the public thinks about public relations: An impression management experiment. *Journalism & Mass Communication Quarterly, 79*(1), 150-171.

(and reputation) online, how else can psychology help us? Firstly, let's talk about anonymity and visibility. We have already touched on these subjects in Chapter 2 in relation to self-disclosure, which we now know is related to confident self-presentation. At one end of the spectrum it's possible to be almost completely invisible on the internet. For instance you can join a forum or listserv and read other people's contributions and conversations without ever taking part in the discussion yourself. At the other end is complete visibility, where you can be identified by your real name, real photo (albeit a flattering one!) and real email address, as you are required to do on LinkedIn.

But in between these two positions, it is possible to provide some identifying information, and to conceal other details. Research into the psychology of online identities reveals many cases of 'managed anonymity'[130], in which internet users have adopted a false identity, sometimes changing gender, age and ethnicity, unknown to the other users with whom they interact. In one very famous case from the 1980s, Alex, a middle-aged male psychologist, adopted a bisexual female persona, whom he called Joan Greene[131]. For several years, Alex pretended to be Joan Greene online, complete with her own carefully constructed history – a woman paralysed and disfigured from a car accident, who, because of her disablement and the fact that she had lost the power of speech, was unable to go out of the house and embarrassed by face-to-face meetings. The online world, then, suited her perfectly. Initially, his motivation was to help other women, but Alex's online alter-ego took on a life of its own. As Joan, he deceived many of the women in internet forums, having online affairs with some of them. 'Joan' even introduced one woman to Alex, who then had a real-life affair with her. In the end, the deceit became too complex to manage, and Alex came clean. You can imagine how the women he had conned felt. And there are other more recent tales of equally

[130] Chester, A. & Bretherton, D. (2007). Impression management and identity online. In: A Joinson, K. McKNenna, T. Postmes & U. Reips (Eds). The Oxford handbook of internet psychology (pp223-236). Oxford. Oxford University Press.
[131] http://www.usemod.com/cgi-bin/mb.pl?AlexAndJoan

bizarre deception, such as the young American woman, 'Kaycee Nicole', a fictitious persona created (and eventually killed off) by her 'mother', Debbie Swenson[132], but not before she had fooled hundreds (maybe even thousands) of people into believing her emotionally compelling online accounts of her struggles against serious illness and adversity. Despite the fact that many people were duped into sending get-well gifts, it seems that Swenson didn't carry out the deception in order to make money. It seems more likely that she did it for the attention associated with having so many people interested in her well-being and hanging on her every word. What the Alex/Joan and Kaycee Nicole stories show is that it is actually pretty easy to pretend to be someone else online, even someone of the opposite gender, and to fool people into believing you. It's also remarkable how quickly a deceit is magnified and grows out of all proportion as a result of the technology.

In virtual worlds like Second Life, adopting a different persona is tolerated, and even expected; in fact in many virtual worlds, because of the use of avatars, you don't even have to be human! Research into the use of avatars, rather than photos, to represent yourself online shows that people who have attractive avatars disclose more information about themselves and are more willing to approach members of the opposite sex online than people who have unattractive avatars, and that people with taller avatars act more confidently when negotiating online than those with shorter avatars[133]. So there seems to be a definite link between how confident you act and how confident you look.

Thankfully, most people you'll meet through social networking sites like Facebook, Twitter and LinkedIn, will be who they say they are. More or less! You need to be aware of the possibility (or perhaps we should say 'probability') that, in the interests of creating as favourable an image as possible, the vast majority of internet users may engage in a little bit of 'home-improvement', such as

[132] http://www.snopes.com/inboxer/hoaxes/kaycee.asp

[133] Yee, N. & Bailenson, J. (2007). The proteus effect: The effect of transformed self-representation on behavior. *Human Communication Research. 33(3).* 271-290.

using photos of themselves from several years ago, in order to appear younger, better looking or slimmer. And to be frank, if psychologists have got it right, we shouldn't expect anything different! Presenting the most positive image of ourselves is simply human nature.

First impressions, radiators and fridges, and the halo effect

As we have suggested above, online interaction can tend to be a little, well, chilly and lacking in human warmth unless we make a concerted effort to appear more affable and welcoming. This is hardly surprising when we consider that in face-to-face interactions we have the opportunity to win people over with our dazzling smile, witty aside or our firm and friendly handshake. Research into the perceived MBTI[134] scores of people who communicate with each other via email suggests that online we tend to come across as more logical, analytical and less people-oriented than we really are, particularly if we have never met the person we're communicating with face-to-face[135]. What's more, studies into the content of what we type when we're online also suggest that we're less likely to make remarks which express understanding, support or solidarity with the people we're communicating with, and more likely to use phrases which express disagreement and different opinions[136]. Not surprisingly, this means that you might inadvertently be creating the impression of being a bit tetchy, impatient and unapproachable, rather than the genial and good-natured person that you really are!

---

[134] The Myers Briggs Type Indicator is a personality-type profiling tool frequently used in business

[135] Fuller, R. (1996). Human-computer-human interaction: How computers affect interpersonal communication. In L.Day & D.K. Kovacs (Eds.). *Computers, communication and mental models.* London: Taylor & Francis.

[136] Hiltz, S.R. & Turoff, M. (1978). *The network nation: Human communication via computer.* Cambridge, MA: The MIT press.

Are you a radiator or a fridge?

Leaving aside the question of physical appearance for a moment, we have other equally unscientific ways of making snap judgements about the people we meet. Whilst these methods might seem illogical, there are sound psychological reasons for jumping to speedy conclusions, not least because it means that we can conserve energy and save our limited cognitive processing power for more important matters! So, what might these psychological short cuts be? Well, for one thing, you need to be aware that simply the level of warmth or coolness you present online actually has a major influence on how other people perceive you. In other words, there is a noticeable 'halo effect', which you can use to your advantage.

In a series of studies into how impressions of people's personalities are formed, psychologist Solomon Asch found that being described as either 'warm' or 'cold' makes a significant difference to other people's perceptions of you. So, for instance, a person who was described as 'intelligent, skilful, industrious, warm, determined practical and cautious' was perceived to be more generous, wise, good-natured, sociable, popular, humane, good-looking (!), altruistic and imaginative than someone described in exactly the same way except the word 'cold' replaced the word 'warm'[137]. Put simply, being seen to be a warm person can have a very positive knock-on effect on the way people perceive your other qualities, so you need to pay particular attention to how you radiate warmth (or not) in your online interactions.

In a follow-up study using real people, students were asked to assess a new male teacher. Before he arrived they were given a short biography of him; half the students had a biography which said the new teacher was 'rather warm', the other half had the same biography except that he was described as 'rather cold'. Interestingly, those students who has been told that the new teacher was warm rated him considerably more favourably than

---

[137] Asch, S. (1946). Forming impressions of personality. *The Journal of Abnormal and Social Psychology*, *41*(3), 258-290.

those who were told he was cold, and more 'warm' than 'cold' students attempted to interact with him[138].

Another important psychological feature which influences our impressions of others, and their impressions of us, is what researchers call the 'primacy effect'. In other words, what we first learn about someone has a greater impact than what we subsequently learn. This was shown to be the case in a study in which people were presented with two lists of adjectives describing a hypothetical person.

	List 1	List 2
1	Intelligent	Envious
2	industrious	Stubborn
3	Impulsive	Critical
4	Critical	Impulsive
5	stubborn	Industrious
6	Envious	Intelligent
	= positive impression	= negative impression

The lists were identical, but shown in a different order. Those people given the first list formed a favourable impression of the hypothetical person, whilst those given the second list formed an unfavourable impression[139]. And the same thing applies in real life too[140].

How accurately people perceive us is also determined by how

[138] Kelley, H.H. (1950). The warm-cold variable in first impressions of people. *Journal of Personality, 18,* 431-439.
[139] Asch, S. (Ibid)
[140] Jones, E.E., Rock, L., Shaver, K.G., Goethals, G.R. & Wand, L.M. (1968). Patterns of performance and ability attribution: An unexpected primacy effect. *Journal of Personality & Social Psychology, 10,* 317-340.

much information we give them. Of course, we disclose ourselves as much by what we say and do as by what we don't say and do. Generally speaking we have more control over verbal than non-verbal behaviour. The factors which influence how much information we give others about ourselves include:

- **Reciprocity** – the more we tell someone about ourselves, the more likely they are to tell us about themselves. Even if we feel that the other person is telling us too much too soon, we're still likely to reveal more about ourselves than we otherwise would[141].
- **Norms or cultural context:** it all depends on the situation we're in. At a dinner party (in the UK at least) it's acceptable to ask (even expected to ask) what job someone does, but you don't ask about their salary or their sex life.
- **Level of trust:** the more we trust someone the more we're likely to disclose information to them.
- **Quality of the relationship:** the more intimate our relationship is, the more likely we are to discuss private or sensitive topics. The reverse is also true[142].
- **Gender:** on the whole women tend to disclose more information about themselves than men do.

So, now that we know that first impressions do indeed count, how can you use this information in your online interactions to create the most favourable impression with other people?

---

[141] *Gouldner,* A.W. (*1960*). The norm of reciprocity: A preliminary statement. *American Sociological Review, 25,* 161-78

[142] Taylor, D., & Altman, I. (1987). Communication in interpersonal relationships: Social penetration processes. *Interpersonal processes: New directions in communication research* (pp. 257-277). Thousand Oaks, CA US: Sage Publications.

Simple ways to radiate warmth!

It almost goes without saying that you need to pay particular attention to the way you write emails or postings online, especially now that you know that, all things being equal, people's internet-based communication is more likely to convey difference of opinion than show support and understanding. Simple things make a difference:

- **Friendly:** use a friendly greeting and addressing the person by name do make a difference to the way your email comes across.
- **Lead-in:** lead the reader into your email, and show warmth: 'Thank you for your email / thanks for calling me this morning, it was good to get an update on the project so far'.
- **Empathy:** show empathy at the start by ask how they are or statements like 'I hope that you are well'. If you are aware they have a partner or children, make an appropriate reference to them too.
- **Emotion:** show some emotion in what you write: 'I'm pleased that.....' or 'I hope that....' or 'I appreciate....'. Of course, don't go over the top or you'll sound insincere, but try practising with one or two of these in your next email.
- **Agreement:** if you're emailing a response to someone, let them know how or where you agree with them – state it explicitly.
- **Sign-off:** finally, always use a full sign off, such as 'kind regards' or 'best wishes'.

Paying attention to what you're writing and the way you're writing it does take a bit more time and thought, but it will pay dividends very quickly. If it's a difficult or sensitive email, we also suggest you give yourself a cooling off period, rather than reply straight away. So think about your reply for 24 hours. If you do need to reply instantly, phone them, as difficult conversations are often better person-to-person.

Using emoticons

Emoticons are those odd keyboard characters strung together to resemble human moods or facial expressions (albeit, those of humans lying on their sides), such as

;-> (for 'winking')
:-o (for 'surprise')
:) (for happy).

As PC software has become more sophisticated, you can now insert some of the basic emoticons into your text as ready-made symbols, rather than create them yourself. They can be very helpful in adding nuances of understanding to what might be otherwise rather blunt text, however psychological research has found that even emoticons are not entirely foolproof.

For instance in one study designed to identify how online disagreements turn into flaming, researchers found that including smiley faces in the text did influence whether or not a message was perceived as a flame, and in those messages which showed tension, the addition of a smiley face reduced the perception of a flame. So far so good! But once the message became personal and antagonistic (i.e. a step up from tension), the addition of a smiley face into the text made matters worse and was more like pouring high octane fuel on the fire than a bucket of cold water.

There is also a need for caution in the use of emoticons, as they are not widely accepted in business and when used in the wrong context can make your email appear child-like. So we would advise that you consider the type of email, and the culture of the organisation before you use them.

Top Tip

Bearing the above advice in mind, use appropriate emoticons to lighten your messages, emails and texts and to portray friendliness and approachability.

As advised in Chapter 3, steer clear of sending any messages that might be construed as flaming. If you receive what you think is an antagonistic, sarcastic or critical email, text or message in an online chat-room, do not reply immediately. It's all too easy to fire off an ill-considered response which inflames the situation and might provoke an even more emotional outburst. So take a break, do something else and wait until your emotion has subsided before you pen your response and hit the 'send' button.

Remember that in a work situation, conflict is easier to resolve by discussing the issues face-to-face or on the phone, than by email. However tempting it might seem, don't get drawn into picking apart the other person's email line by line. Life's too short. It's more likely to prolong the disagreement than resolve it. And don't get drawn in by using the 'he/she started it' justification. Leave this to the kids in the playground.

;->

So now that we've thought about how the emotional tone and content of what we write online affects whether we appear to be warm and approachable, rather than cold and distant, what other features of online communication do you need to be aware of?

The importance of being Ernest

One of us has just recently become a parent for the first time, and yes we spent months with our spouse pouring over the 'Bumper Book of Baby's Names', trying to find ones we could agree on, which suited our surname, and which the grandparents wouldn't hold up their hands in horror at (we went for Beatrice by the way!). That's probably something that 99% of new parents go through. Our choice might have been made a whole lot quicker had we thought about the characteristics that are psychologically associated with various first names; for example, there is research to show that 'Katherine' and 'Alexander' are considered significantly more successful, ambitious, intelligent, confident and creative than 'Sadie' and 'Rufus'[143], and that 'Holly' is outgoing, fun, popular and good-looking, Andy and Chris are names associated with more pleasant temperaments, whereas poor old Rick and Kevin are not.

So not only is your name an important part of your identity, psychological research shows that it can also influence other people's expectations of you, and alters their behaviour towards you. In a study done in the 1970s[144], researchers showed that the same school essays were graded higher if the teachers thought they were written by children with attractive names (in this case 'David', 'Michael', 'Karen' and 'Lisa') than when the teachers thought they were written by children with unattractive names ('Elmer', 'Hubert', 'Bertha' and 'Adelle'). And it doesn't just stop there. In the UK, research cited in the *New Scientist* has shown that doctors may discriminate against patients and give them different diagnoses depending on whether or not they have an attractive name[145]. In this case, 464 British psychiatrists were asked to assess (based on a one page description) a 24 year old man, who had attacked a train conductor. Over 75% of them were sympathetic to the man when he was named 'Matthew': they suggested that he might be suffering from schizophrenia and that he was in need of medical attention. But astonishingly, they were far less sympathetic when he was named 'Wayne'. In fact, 'Wayne' was twice as likely as 'Matthew' to be diagnosed as a malingerer, a substance abuser or suffering from

---

[143] Mehrabian, A. (2001). Characteristics attributed to individuals on the basis of their first names. *Genetic, Social & General Psychology Monographs, 127*(1), 59

[144] Harari, H. & McDavid, J.W. (1973). Teachers' expectations and name stereotypes. Journal of Educational Psychology, 65, 222-225.

[145] Dr L Birmingham, cited in Adler (2000). *Pigeonholed.* New Scientist. 167(2258). 38-41. See BBC News http://news.bbc.co.uk/1/hi/health/818730.stm

a personality disorder.

We're not proposing that you rush out and get a deed poll form (in fact, you can do this online now anyway[146]), but you do need to be aware how important your email address or your username is to the creation of your online identity. After all, it's frequently the first thing that people see when they interact with you for the first time on the internet, via email or in a chat room or forum. As mentioned above there's a significant body of research into the psychology of proper names and the personality characteristics that people attribute to others on the basis of their first names[147], whereas studies on the psychology of usernames or email addresses are still pretty rare.

If you're employed, the chances are that you won't have a choice about the email address assigned to you. It will be something along the lines of:

firstname.lastname@youremployer.com.

But if you're self-employed, or a frequenter of internet chat-rooms, you'll be able to choose your own name (within the constraints of the software), and for the sake of impression management, it's important that you pick wisely.

It's claimed that people often don't consider the impact that their domain name or username makes[148], but if you stop to think about it for even a moment, you'll realise that this is as important a feature of your personal branding as the way you dress or the content of your website. For instance, could you take seriously a freelance business consultant called Steve Jones whose email address was Steve.Jones1969@hotmail.com or SteveJones2@Tesco.net?

Yet both of us know people whose business cards present email addresses like this. Using this type of account is absolutely fine for

[146] http://www.ukdps.co.uk/

[147] Mehrabian, A. (2001). Characteristics attributed to individuals on the basis of their first names. *Genetic, Social and General Psychology Monographs. 127(1),* 59-88.

[148] Wallace, P. (1999). *The psychology of the internet.* Cambridge, UK. Cambridge University Press.

personal email and communication, but if you want to create a convincing business presence, you need to look like you're serious by registering a credible domain name (usually linked to your website, if you have one).

Similarly, where you have a choice, you need to put some thought into the name that goes to the left of the '@' symbol. As Patricia Wallace, author of The Psychology of the Internet points out, people are not going to take 'tufdude888@aol.com', 'FoxyLady@flash.net' or 'LoveChik' seriously[149]!

A study of internet usernames suggests that they fall into essentially six different categories:[150]

Category	%
Names which relate to or describe the self e.g. 'shydude'	45.0%
Names related to the medium or to technology e.g. 'Pentium'	16.9%
Names related to flora, fauna, objects e.g. 'froggy'	15.6%
Play on words and sounds e.g. 'uh-uh'	11.3%
People using their real name	7.8%
Names related to figures in literature, films, fairytales and famous people e.g. 'madhatter'	6.1%
Provocative names or those related to sex e.g. 'sexpot'	3.9%
Total (more than 100% because some names fit more than one category)	106.6%

Unless you're working in the technology field, where outlandish or unusual usernames tend to be more acceptable, in reality the

[149] Wallace p20-21.

[150] Bechar-Israeli, H. (1996). From <Bonehead> to <cLoNehEAd>: Nicknames, play and identity on internet relay chat. *Journal of Computer-Mediated Communication*, 2.: http://jcmc.indiana.edu/vol1/issue2/bechar.html

best option is to use a version of your real name. You should also be aware that you 'grow into' your chosen username; in this same study, researchers found that people quickly identify with their username and as a result , they don't often change it, even though this is usually very easy to do. So if you've been contributing to an online chat-room about fly-fishing with the username 'pickledherring', that's fine, but think carefully before you transport 'pickledherring' to a forum or user group about critical incident management!

In Facebook, theoretically you're supposed to use your real name, although many people opt for a nickname or an abbreviation when they first create their account. If at some later stage you decide you want to change it, it's very easy to do; you just need to go into your account, go to settings and next to your name, click on 'change'. Simple!

Top Tip

If you want to create a good impression, don't use a free domain name that comes from your broadband provider (such as hotmail, aol or BT) as your main business email address.

Instead contact a local hosting company who will be able to provide you with a tailor-made URL. You can check out the availability of URLs first using a WHOIS website such as :

http://www.uwhois.com/domains.html

URL hosting is extremely competitively priced, and costs from as little as £5 a year. It will take a hosting company a matter of days to set up.

There really is no excuse!

Minding your PC Ps & Qs

Although the World Wide Web is also often portrayed in the popular media as weird and wild, a place where absolutely anything goes, it didn't really take very long before certain rules were established to help regulate online behaviour and communication. These rules are commonly referred to as 'netiquette'. In 1995, the Internet Engineering Task Force (IETF), a body which develops and promotes internet standards, issued a document (known in the trade as a 'Request For Comments', or RFC), outlining the basic rules of internet behaviour[151]. Although this RFC could now be considered pre-historic in technology terms, the vast majority of these original guidelines are still applicable today, so we have reproduced the most relevant ones below. If you want to come across as knowledgeable and approachable as well as professional, we suggest you take a look at these guidelines:

Netiquette for Email

- Unless you have your own Internet access through an Internet provider, be sure to check with your employer about ownership of electronic mail.
- Unless you are using an encryption device, you should assume that email on the Internet is not secure. Never put in an email anything you would not put on a postcard.
- Respect the copyright on material that you reproduce. Almost every country has copyright laws.
- If you are forwarding or re-posting a message you've received, do not change the wording. If the message was a personal message to you and you are re-posting to a group, you should ask permission first. You may shorten

[151] Author: Sally Hambridge, Intel Corporation, http://www.faqs.org/ftp/rfc/pdf/rfc1855.txt.pdf

the message and quote only relevant parts, but be sure you give proper attribution.

- Never send chain letters via email.
- A good rule of thumb: Be conservative in what you send and liberal in what you receive. You should not send heated messages ('flames') even if you are provoked. On the other hand, you shouldn't be surprised if you get flamed. It's prudent not to respond..
- In general, it's a good idea to at least check all your emails before responding. Sometimes a person who asks you for help (or clarification) will send another message which effectively says 'Never Mind'. Also make sure that any message you respond to was directed to you. You might be 'cc'd rather than the primary recipient.
- Be careful when addressing email. There are addresses which may go to a group but the address looks like it is just one person. Know to whom you are sending.
- Watch cc's when replying. Don't continue to include people if the messages have become a two-way conversation.
- Remember that people with whom you communicate are located across the globe. If you send an email to which you want an immediate response, the person receiving it might be at home asleep when it arrives. Give them a chance to wake up, come to work, and log in before assuming the email didn't arrive or that they don't care.
- Remember that the recipient is a human being whose culture, language, and humour have different points of reference from your own. Remember that date formats, measurements, and idioms may not travel well. Be especially careful with sarcasm.

- Use mixed case. UPPER CASE LOOKS AS IF YOU'RE SHOUTING.
- Use emoticons to indicate tone of voice, but use them sparingly. Don't assume that the inclusion of a smiley will make the recipient happy with what you say or wipe out an otherwise insulting comment.
- If you include a signature keep it short. Rule of thumb is no longer than four lines.
- Don't send large amounts of unsolicited information to people.

Guidelines for effective communication on mailing lists (aka listservs) and top tips for making your emails compelling can be found in the Appendix.

Mea culpa?

'Oops, I did it again...'
Britney Spears

So now we've covered the basics of online courtesy, there's no excuse for getting it wrong. Except that we're all human, and however hard we try, we all make mistakes occasionally! Unfortunately there are no hard and fast rules when it comes to online apologies, because it really does depend on circumstances. As you can imagine, sometimes a quick, concise message expressing your sincere regret will be enough, whereas at other times, nothing short of a heartfelt apology will do. But there is also a third option, and that is to ignore the error or *faux pas* and do absolutely nothing at all, on the basis of the 'least said, soonest mended' principle.

This latter option is probably the easiest and the most convenient for you the wrongdoer. For one thing you don't have to put time and thought into crafting a suitable message; you can simply bury your head in the sand and hope the incident, whatever it is, gets forgotten quickly. It's what in business is called 'moving on', i.e. don't expect an apology, just get over it.

But when a misdemeanour is such that an apology is deserved, you need to know how to go about it. According to Barbara Kellerman writing in the *Harvard Business Review*[152], apologising effectively is rarely a simple act. Through her study of various public apologies from business leaders, she has come up with a list of five elements which together constitute a 'good apology':

- Acknowledging the mistake or wrongdoing
- Accepting responsibility
- Expressing regret
- Providing assurance that the offence won't be repeated
- Timing it well (often easier said than done!).

Because sincere apologies are an admission of guilt, there is an increasing tendency for business people to avoid making them publicly to avoid the likelihood of being hoist by their own petard. In some ultra-competitive businesses, even the slightest whiff of a mistake is enough to start the vultures circling overhead. That said, some legal experts suggest that it is precisely the failure to admit a mistake and apologise for it which more often leads to legal action. In order to overcome this issue, some American states have enacted a law which allows healthcare providers and medical professionals to make an apology and express sympathy without this being taken as an admission of liability in a court of law.

There are some very well-known examples of how the refusal of business leaders to own up to mistakes then creates huge problems for themselves and their organisations later on. One such instance occurred when chairman and CEO of Coca-Cola, M. Douglas Ivester, dismissed customer complaints of nausea and headaches after drinking Coke products as unfounded. This refusal to listen to customers eventually damaged his professional reputation and,

---

[152] Kellerman, B. (2006). 'When should a leader apologize and when not?.' *Harvard Business Review, 84(4),* 72-81

Kellerman suggests, led to his stepping down after just two years in the post.

Another, which has also become a classic in management text books as an example of how not to communicate with your staff, is the email written by Neal Patterson, co-founder and CEO of American healthcare company Cerner. In 2001, Patterson, infuriated by what he saw as employees' lack of commitment (i.e. the car park being less than full at 8am and 5pm) sent an email to his top 400 managers. His tirade has gone down in 'PR disaster' history; the New York Times reported[153]:

> *"We are getting less than 40 hours of work from a large number of our K.C.-based EMPLOYEES. The parking lot is sparsely used at 8 a.m.; likewise at 5 p.m. As managers – you either do not know what your EMPLOYEES are doing; or you do not CARE. You have created expectations on the work effort which allowed this to happen inside Cerner, creating a very unhealthy environment. In either case, you have a problem and you will fix it or I will replace you.*
>
> *"NEVER in my career have I allowed a team which worked for me to think they had a 40-hour job. I have allowed YOU to create a culture which is permitting this. NO LONGER."*

Mr Patterson went on to list six potential punishments, including laying off 5 percent of the staff and installing a clocking-in system. "Hell will freeze over," he vowed, before he would dole out more employee benefits. The parking lot would be his yardstick of success, he said. It should be "substantially full" at 7:30 a.m. and 6:30 p.m. on weekdays and half full on Saturdays.

> *"You have two weeks," he concluded ominously. "Tick tock."*

Patterson's email found its way onto the internet and in particular

[153] http://www.nytimes.com/2001/04/05/business/stinging-office-memo-boomerangs-chief-executive-criticized-after-upbraiding.html?n=Top/Reference/Times%20Topics/Subjects/C/Computers%20and%20the%20Internet&pagewanted=all

onto a Yahoo bulletin board used by Cerner's investors. Rather than own up to his mistake and try to put the matter right, Patterson and Cerner's PR team ignored it, with the catastrophic result that the value of company's stock plummeting 22% in 3 days, wiping $270m off its market capitalisation, and $28million from Patterson's own portfolio.

Patterson did eventually see error of his ways, and apologised to staff [apparently asking them to keep his email of contrition for 'internal dissemination purposes only' – it never made it into the public domain]. Fortunately for him, Cerner's share price did eventually recover[154]. And he's still the CEO. But be warned!

Giving as good as you get. Or the law of karma on the net

In online terms, interactions need to be mutually advantageous, that is, you need to consider what you can do for others as well as (or even before) being concerned about what they can do for you. A great example of this is how to get your messages forwarded on Twitter, which is a fantastic way of positively building your reputation.

Impression management on Twitter: the Re-Tweet

'Re-tweeting' (aka RT) is simply the process of forwarding someone else's tweet to all your followers on Twitter. The reason you want to increase the number of times your tweets are re-tweeted is because this is measure of your value to others. In fact, some social media gurus like Guy Kawasaki[155] and Dan Zarella[156] go as far as to say the number of RTs you get is a more accurate measure of your value, since it's actually relatively easy to gain followers (as in 'follow a lot of people and they tend to follow you back'), whereas to get RT'd you actually do need to be tweeting things that other people find interesting, helpful, funny, fascinating or otherwise worthy of note.

---

[154] http://findarticles.com/p/articles/mi_m0FXS/is_6_80/ai_75916203/

[155] http://blogs.openforum.com/2009/02/18/how-to-get-retweeted/

[156] http://mashable.com/2009/02/17/twitter-retweets/

So what do you need to do to increase the number of RTs you get on Twitter? Here are our top five suggestions:

1. Be interesting. In other words, answer the right question, which according to Kawasaki is 'What's interesting?' not 'What are you doing?' We whole-heartedly agree with him – see our section on Twitter in Chapter 2. Unless you are Stephen Fry or Barack Obama, very few followers will be interested to hear about the minutiae of your daily existence.

   There are many Twitter users who do answer the 'What are you doing?' question, but by and large, they're using Twitter just to keep in touch with close family and friends, and not as a marketing, branding, PR or change tool.

   So if you want to increase the number of RTs you get, make sure you write about things which other Twitter users will find useful in some way, and will want to tell their followers about.

2. Be educational. Twitter users like to learn new things, so write about how to do something. This is where, as a professional quantity surveyor, commercial lawyer, dentist, crossword puzzle-solver, parent or gardener, you can give full rein to sharing your knowledge with others. Kawasaki recommends starting your tweet with the words 'How to', or 'The Art of...' in order to get people hooked.

3. Be useful. The internet doesn't have a Yellow Pages directory, so there are plenty of websites out there that you will have come across that other people haven't. So providing links to them in your tweets is one way of sharing a lot of information using a very small number of characters. You can provide links to absolutely anything, blogs, news sites, photos, organisations, companies etc, but do make sure they're genuinely useful or entertaining and not simply advertising for your own blog, or for your best friend's company. 'One way to definitely put people off and irritate them is to constantly 'sell' your business', says Twitter-user, Yang-May Ooi, 'the key thing is to be yourself – a whole person and not a sales person'.

4. Be human and be yourself. This isn't the same thing as 'baring all' you understand. Remember what we said in Chapter 3 about the tendency to reveal more about yourself online than you would face-to-face.

   You're allowed to use humour of course, just make sure you do it carefully; in-jokes can, of course, exclude others.

5. Ask for help. Finally, don't be afraid to ask people to RT your message if you want to get it out to a wider audience. Providing your tweet is interesting, most people will be happy to help.

In short, as long as you're adding value through Twitter rather than idly passing the time of day, the chances are that you'll be able to build up a credible reputation as a professional worth following in no time at all.

A potential downside of self-promotion

This being a book about the psychology of internet networking means that we have to consider the drawbacks as well as the advantages. Self-promotion is a double-edged sword and, it turns out, for women more so than for men. Psychology research shows that people perceive self-promotion in men and women very differently. Self-promoting women (e.g. those who speak in a direct, self confident manner, highlight their accomplishments and make internal rather than external attributions for their success) get higher ratings of professional competence than women who do not promote themselves, but they are likely to be viewed as less socially attractive, especially by other women. Paradoxically, in experiments, women were less likely to prefer hiring a self-promoting woman, even when their own success depended on it. Researchers have suggested that this is linked to cultural norms, where even in the 21st Century, women are expected to be modest, self-effacing and feminine, rather than pushy, independent or self-confident[157].

---

[157] Rudman, L. (1998). Self-promotion as a risk factor for women: The costs and benefits of

So for women there is a Catch-22 situation here, where they can miss out on opportunities if they don't push themselves forward, but they can be discriminated against (especially by other women) if they do.

No wonder that effective self-promotion for women has been called 'a difficult and demanding balancing act akin to driving over rough terrain while keeping one hand on the wheel and the other reassuringly on passengers' backs'[158]!

counterstereotypical impression management. *Journal of Personality and Social Psychology*, *74*(3), 629-645.

[158] Rudman, L., & Glick, P. (1999). Feminized management and backlash toward agentic women: The hidden costs to women of a kinder, gentler image of middle managers. *Journal of Personality & Social Psychology*, *77*(5), 1004-1010.

5

Realising the business and career benefits of personal networking

In this chapter we focus on other ways of promoting yourself (and your business) online, and on getting you familiar with networking as it typically happens in the real world. The reason for the former is that using social networking sites like Twitter and LinkedIn is not the only way to get your message out there; you have other choices, and actually you may decide that a multi-format approach is more appropriate. Whilst you may be quite comfortable with using social networks and see the transition to using them for work purposes as no big deal, you will meet plenty of other managers and professionals who don't know their Facebook from their Flickr[159], or who much prefer to stick with more traditional approaches to networking, so you need to be comfortable that you know how that works too. Whether you're a member of Gen Y or not, the advice given in this chapter will useful for you.

---

[159] http://www.flickr.com

Blogging

Baking your half-baked ideas[160]

According to Technorati, the world's leading blog search engine, whether we like it or not, blogs are now pervasive and part of our everyday lives. Although the size of the blogosphere, and its worldwide readership, varies depending which technology expert you speak to, the number of blogs indexed by Technorati is evidence enough that blogging is here to stay:

Number of blogs...	
...indexed by Technorati since 2002	133 million
...posted in last 120 days	7.4 million
...posted in last 7 days	1.5 million
...posted in last 24 hours	900,000

Whilst these numbers might be pretty scary to the average non-blogger, and you may be thinking what's the point of launching yet another novice blog into the 'A list' ocean of popular, well-read and highly-rated expert blogs, the reasons for creating and writing your own blog are pretty compelling. But before we talk about why blogging is a vital personal and business promotion tool, let's just take a quick tour through the birth and evolution of blogs as we know them.

The first-ever blog has been attributed to Justin Hall, then student at Swarthmore College, Pennsylvania, who in January 1994 began writing online about his personal life: you can still read some of his original website[161]. People typically think of blogs as being

[160] Technorati: http://technorati.com/blogging/state-of-the-blogosphere/the-what-and-why-of-blogging/

[161] http://links.net/vita/web/start/original.html. Fifteen years later, Hall is still blogging here: http://links.net/

online diaries or journals, maintained by individuals, but nowadays corporate and group blogging make a significant contribution to the blogosphere. Since 1998, the number of blogs has increased every year: in their 2008 report, Technorati claim to be indexing 120,000 new blogs every day, that's one new blog every 1.4 seconds. So why do people bother? What is it about blogging that captures the imaginations of so many people across the world?

According to Technorati's latest survey, people blog for many reasons, most commonly:

To speak my mind on areas which interest me	79%
To share my expertise and experience with others	73%
To meet and connect with like-minded people	62%
To update friends and family on my life	32%
To feature or get published in traditional media	26%
To make money or supplement my income	24%
To enhance my resume	21%
To attract clients to my business	14%

The above statistics suggest that adding their voice to the conversation is more important to bloggers than expanding their businesses or enhancing their reputation, but that's not to say that these can't or shouldn't be your goals. Indeed, we've spoken to many business people, as well as freelancers and consultants, who write their own blogs, about the benefits to them as professionals. They're passionate supporters of blogging as a tool for enhancing reputation, building relationships with existing and potential clients, increasing business credibility, and improving their visibility in their chosen field.

Evan Jones LLP: www.evansjones.co.uk

David Jones, a Chartered Surveyor and partner at Evans Jones LLP in Cheltenham, Gloucestershire, makes a very compelling argument for the power of blogging to enhance business. Jones added a blog to his partnership website[162] in 2006, and since then has not looked back. The blog created interest amongst existing Evans Jones' clients and brought in significant contracts from new clients looking for business partners who could clearly demonstrate their professional expertise. At the same time it raised the profile of the existing Evans Jones website and assisted the practice in moving from a local practice to one which now regularly works nationwide.

Jones says, *'When we decided to launch the blog it was a bit of a leap of faith and I had to persuade my partners that it would be worth the investment in time and money. Of course we didn't get the content right straight away, but very quickly we learnt what works. Chartered surveying, like many other professions, is changing quickly, so we have to keep our clients up to date on new rules and regulations, and the blog is an ideal way to do that; it's an easily managed section of our website which enables us to react very quickly to the ever-changing business environment. We got very positive feedback from clients, who found they could rely on our knowledge and expertise in the professional field to keep them up to date on issues and solutions. In all, we're really pleased that we made the decision to set up the blog. The Evans Jones partnership has been benefiting from it ever since.'*

If that's not enough to convince you of the power of blogging to enhance your professional reputation and grow your business,

[162] http://www.evansjones.co.uk/

here's what Yang-May Ooi, best-selling author[163] and blogger[164] has to say on the subject: *'A blog offers you an excellent opportunity to share your expertise, if you offer professional services, and your passion about your product or sector, if you provide products and other goods. It is also a space where you can make yourself available and engage with your customers and other stakeholders to discuss issues and news relevant to your business or sector.'* Blogging has made a huge difference to Ooi's professional career; she explains, *'Blogging has raised my profile as a writer. Through my blog, FusionView.co.uk, I have had several opportunities to write for print and online journals. I have also made a range of contacts and friends in the literary community and was invited to speak and give readings in Malaysia entirely through a network of lit bloggers that I met through blogging. I started by trying out blogging on the free Blogger.com site but soon invested in paying a web designer to design both my blog and also my writing website -- this turned out to be one of the best investments I've made as it has helped add a 'wow factor' to my online presence as well as ensuring that my blog is seen as that of a professional writer and not just one of millions of blogs by amateur, would-be writers. The credibility I built up as a blogger to be taken seriously led directly to my being invited to co-author the social media chapters of the business book International Communications Strategy.'*

Ooi is keen to emphasise that social media are all about relationship-building. She continues, *'Personally, blogging, Twitter and other forms of social media have enriched my friendships with my real-world friends who are also engaged online. Twitter and Facebook as well as instant messaging/chat on Skype or Google Talk offer similar opportunities to pass the time of day with trivialities which in themselves are nothing but over time help deepen and develop relationships. When we do meet up in person, but we don't have to spend the initial time we are together catching up with what*

---

[163] International Communications Strategy: Developments in Cross-Cultural Communications, PR and Social Media (2009) – Kogan Page Ltd (co-authored with Sylvia Cambie). The Flame Tree (1998) – Hodder & Stoughton Ltd. Mindgame(2000) – Coronet Books.

[164] http://www.fusionview.co.uk/

has been going on in the last few months but instead can delve deeper into things that we already know about each others' lives.'

Having looked at the advantages of blogging to you as a professional, we now turn to the practicalities: what do you need to do, how do you do it, and when?

How to set up a blog

Setting up a blog is incredibly easy; there are several off-the-shelf tools that you can use, such as Wordpress[165] or Blogger[166]. All you need to do is choose your blog host, open up an account at their website, pick a name for your blog and you're ready to start blogging. It really couldn't be simpler.

You can, of course, integrate a blog into a pre-existing website (as Evans Jones did in the example given above), or set up both together, although unless you have some website design and build expertise you'd probably be better off doing the latter, or find a local expert to help you. If you're on a tight budget, don't forget that IT students are a good source of expertise and are often looking for a little paid work to help top up their college fees.

How to be content with your content

Once you have the format and design of your blog worked out, the next thing to consider is what exactly you're going to write. Now assuming your goal in becoming a member of the blogerati is to showcase your professional expertise, you might like to start by thinking about how you're going to differentiate what you write from the other blogs about marketing / photography / retailing or whatever your specialist subject is. We've put together a list of Golden Rules, i.e. those that every blogger should adhere to.

---

[165] www.wordpress.com

[166] www.blogger.com

The Golden Rules

- Entertain your readers. Dull content will be the death of your blog, so make sure it's engaging.
- Educate and inform readers – give them something new, or new slants on existing stories. Like 'how to' Tweets, 'how to' blog postings are always popular.
- Inspire your readers: tell them motivating, thought-provoking stories.
- Be humorous – your postings don't have to be laugh-out-loud funny every time, but do allow your sense of humour to shine through.
- Challenge your readers – you don't have to give them everything on a plate; make them think about the subject in question. You can be provocative too, just make sure it's in keeping with the overall professional image that you are trying to create.
- Make it memorable! You want people to come back to your blog and also to recommend it to their friends and colleagues.
- Finally, ask them for their feedback. Depending on the type of blog you write, you may not always get comments, but that's not to say that your blog isn't hitting the mark, especially if you're writing in a professional field. There are many software packages available which track your blog statistics; it's well worth using one so that you get a sense of the impact you're making.

All of the above will develop naturally as you practise and hone your own personal writing style, so there's nothing like getting on with it and starting to write a couple of posts. If you're feeling a bit under-confident, have a look again at our advice in Chapter 3 about getting out of your comfort zone and taking small steps. You may find it helpful to ask friends and colleagues for feedback on what you've written (even if they don't write their comments publicly) or you could consider contacting another blogger or a coach to ask for their help.

Additionally there are a number of other practical guidelines which will help you quickly develop your blog into an effective marketing and publicity tool for you (and, if you're self-employed, for your business too).

- Post frequently – it doesn't really matter if it's hourly, daily, weekly or monthly as long as you're pretty consistent. Many new bloggers make the assumption that they can wait for the inspiration to take them, which means that their blogs may go for weeks or months without any updates at all. If you're not disciplined enough to keep to a regular schedule, try to write some extra 'filler' posts in advance when you have some time on your hands; you can then use them for the times when your muse deserts you. BUT

- At the same time, don't blog just for the sake of it. Every post should be for a reason, and that reason should always be in line with your overall goal – to enhance your reputation. Writing half-heartedly on your chosen subject will not do the trick. That's not to say that every posting needs to be a Pulitzer prize winner, we're all human after all. But effective blogging does require some effort, and sticking power.

- Be original – don't repeat a story just because everyone else has, even if it's a good one. If it's too important a story to ignore, try to find your own, original slant on it. If you refer to someone else's work (for example, in another blog, or use their images from Flickr.com[167] to illustrate your posting) then link to it and always attribute it.

[167] www.flickr.com

- Use your judgment. As we have already pointed out in previous chapters, it's much easier to bare your soul on the internet than you might think, and pouring out your heart to readers about sleeping with the boss's son or daughter or how you left a confidential client file on the train to London last night might seem like a good idea at 3am after a skinful, but confessions like this always look far less appealing in the cold light of morning.
- Proofread everything you write at least once before you post it, and always use the spellchecker, even if you don't think you need to. It's surprisingly easy for mistakes to creep in especially if you've been working on the same posting for a while. And a misplaced or missing 'not' can change the message entirely!
- Finally, keep to the point. There are some who are masters of the shaggy dog story, but blogs are rarely the place for them. People's attention spans online can be remarkably short and readers may be turned off by what they see as longwinded, unfocused or rambling posts.

Publicise your blog

Of course there's little point in devoting precious time to writing a blog it you're then going to keep it all to yourself, so you do need to spend some time thinking about how to publicise it. First of all you will need to get your blog 'listed' on internet search engines like Google, so that when people 'google' you and your blog, it will be found. You can manually submit your blog address to Google and Yahoo. Bear in mind that submitting your blog to a search engine doesn't mean that you'll suddenly get lots of readers; it simply means that they can find you if they search specifically for you.

But getting search engines to list your website when people don't know about you is why many website owners employ Search Engine Optimisation (SEO) consultants, i.e. people with the technical knowledge and expertise about how search engines and directories index and rank websites and who can therefore re-design existing websites to make them appear higher up in the list of search engine rankings (i.e. on page 1 or 2, rather than on page 10 where they're much less likely to be found), and therefore increase the amount of visitors they receive. The key thing you need to know about search engine rankings is that the way it is done literally changes from day to day to prevent websites manipulating them, so there is some skill involved in getting your blog or website listed at the top. But fortunately, keywords aren't everything. As successful blogger Yang-May Ooi[168] points out, 'A blog and other 'Web 2.0' applications offer the opportunity for regularly updated content which will help raise your profile online without heavy reliance on keywords'. So there is definitely a lot to be said for writing frequent blog postings, since new, fresh content is one of the things that search engines thrive on. Setting a daily or weekly schedule of writing and posting should help to ensure that your blog appears in the first couple of pages of a Google search, without spending thousands on an SEO consultant.

Since Google's ranking works on the basis of links, one of the most effective ways to raise your profile (and, at the same time, the ranking of your blog) on Google is to get other bloggers and website owners to link to your blog or website. Two simple ways to encourage this are to put a blogroll on your blog, and to leave comments on other people's blogs. Both of these work on the reciprocity principle, whereby if you blogroll another blog, or leave comments on their site, they may do the same in return.

Before we leave this section, it's also worth bearing in mind that you can, and should, utilise the power of your social networks to help you publicise your blog. Both Facebook and LinkedIn allow you to list your blog on your profile page, and on both sites you can import your blog so that the posts automatically appear here too. You should consider doing this, since it exposes you to new readers without any extra effort:

How to publicise your blog on Facebook:

In Facebook, go to the Applications section which is on the left-hand side of the menu bar at the bottom of the page.

[168] www.fusionview.co.uk

In the list of Applications which appears on the left-hand side, click on 'Notes'.

You will then be taken to the Notes page. You will see on the right-hand side a box called 'Notes Settings', and an option to 'Import a blog'. Simply click on this option, insert the URL for your blog, tick the box which says you have the right to allow Facebook to reproduce your blog content, and click 'Import'.

How to publicise your blog on LinkedIn:

If your blog uses Wordpress software, you can also publicise it on your LinkedIn profile, as follows:

In LinkedIn, select the Applications section which is on the left-hand menu

From the list of Applications, select Wordpress

Assuming that you already have your blog's URL listed on your LinkedIn profile page, click on 'Add Application'.

The pros and cons of blogging at work

As we suggested above, you need to use your judgement when considering which work-related stories to feature in your blog; if you're currently employed, your contract of employment will specifically forbid you from divulging sensitive company information, such as details of client contracts, budgets and product or service components, but few refer to blogging. Unless you're being wholeheartedly positive, common sense says that you should avoid referring to colleagues by name, or in any way that could allow them to be identified publicly. Telling your mates down the pub about your colleagues' indiscretions at the office Christmas party is one thing; telling the world about them on your blog (or on your Facebook Wall, for that matter) is an entirely different matter.

You should also be careful about blogging on company time. In the same way that your employer may have a problem with you using Facebook during office hours, the same may be true of blogging. Don't forget that blog postings, like Facebook messages, have a date and time stamp. Many a blogger has come unstuck by ignoring this simple fact.

There are many now infamous cases, of bloggers who have overstepped the mark, and lost their jobs as a result of writing indiscreetly and/or on company time, for example:

- Heather Armstrong was sacked in 2002 for writing some pretty unsavoury things about her job and bosses on her blog, Dooce.com[169]. It's not all bad news however; seven years on she's still writing the blog, and apparently she makes enough money from it that neither she nor her husband need to work. The incident is so well-known that the term 'dooced' has entered common web parlance meaning to be fired for something you've posted on your blog.

- Matthew Brown, a 28 year old supervisor, was fired from a Toronto Starbucks in 2004 for posting comments about the coffee chain, its customers and managers on his personal blog.[170]

- Catherine Sanderson, who blogged under the pseudonym of 'La Petite Anglaise', was fired from her job as a secretary of the accounting firm Dixon Wilson in 2006 for allegedly bringing the firm into disrepute. As it happens, she also came out of the incident smelling of roses: she successfully sued them for wrongful dismissal and went on to sign a major publishing deal as a result.[171]

- Joe (surname unknown), who was fired in 2005 from the Edinburgh branch of Waterstones, where he'd worked for eleven years since graduating, because he had occasionally referred unfavourably to his work in his satirical blog, The Woolamaloo Gazette[172].

---

[169] http://www.dooce.com/archives/daily/02_26_2002.html
[170] http://blogcritics.org/culture/article/employee-fired-by-starbucks-over-blog/
[171] http://www.independent.co.uk/arts-entertainment/books/reviews/petite-anglaise-by-catherine-sanderson-798701.html
[172] http://www.woolamaloo.org.uk/2005/01/those-who-profess-to-favor-freedom-and.htm

And there are, it seems, quite a few others.[173] So the moral of the story seems to be, think twice before you criticise your boss and co-workers in a public medium. For a quieter life, stick to lambasting them when you're down the pub.

Podcasting

'Podcasting is to listening as blogging is to reading' is one way of looking at the art of podcasting, but in fact this content-delivery medium is a whole lot more than that. Despite the name, it's not the case that you need an iPod to listen to a podcast; you can do so on any mobile phone, PC or MP3 player.

Many bloggers include podcasts in their blogs for readers to download at any point; it makes a good contrast to always having written or visual content; some people are naturally better speakers than they are writers so if this is the case for you, podcasting might be a better bet than blogging. Clearly, podcasting is also good for those blog subscribers whose preferred learning style is auditory. But the problem with straight audio blogs is that readers have to check regularly for new MP3 files, and if they want to listen to them on the move, they have to download them to an MP3 player (such as an iPod) by hand. Nowadays podcast content can be delivered and synched to a portable MP3 player automatically, which makes the whole process so much simpler. And there is more than enough great audio content (music, comedy, drama, social and political commentary, you name it) on the web to fill your MP3 player many times over, in fact there is so much available that you need never listen to a traditional radio station ever again.

A podcast is a file of audio content distributed over the internet; so if you had a mind to, you could create your own 'radio plays' or record your own songs and have them distributed on the web rather than on the radio. The big benefit is that whereas a radio station audience is limited by the power of the radio wave transmitter, the internet has no such restrictions – so as long as

[173] http://morphemetales.wordpress.com/2009/01/29/statistics-on-fired-bloggers/

there is broadband access, your podcast can just as easily be listened to by someone in Japan as in Jamaica.

Remember that whilst the internet may still seem a bit like the Wild West, and isn't subject to the same rules at the radio airwaves, you're still responsible for the content of your podcasts, so you should play strictly by the rules concerning using licensed music and songs, any materials that have been copyrighted, and recording people's conversations without their permission.

How to create a podcast

So what do you need in order to create a great podcast? Although some people wouldn't dream of trying this without the latest state-of-the-art equipment, basically all you need is some audio-recording software, a microphone and an audio card which allows you to run the hardware, and which most computers already have built-in. The software, such as Soundrecorder or iTunes might come pre-installed on your PC or Mac, but if not you can you can easily and quickly download some free, open-source software from the web, such as Audacity[174] or Easypodcast[175]. If you're new to podcasting, we recommend that you write a script or at least some notes about the subject of your podcast to keep you on track, unless you're an accomplished ad-libber.

How to record a podcast

Prepare notes about what you want to talk about. If you're not a natural or proficient reader of scripts, notes written in bullet point format work better than a word-for-word account of what you want to say, otherwise you risk appearing stilted and unnatural, and your listeners may be distracted by the rustling papers. We recommend you keep it to about 10-15 minutes, unless you're already a real pro or are capturing a conversation or interview. Monologues can be difficult to listen to for any length of time if you don't have a

[174] http://audacity.sourceforge.net/
[175] http://www.easypodcast.com/

mellifluous voice. You might think this isn't very long, but on the basis most people speak at an average of 200 words a minute, that would be about 6-7 sides of A4 text.

Set up your PC/Mac and microphone.

Open your recording software, click 'record' and talk through your notes / bullet points, and click 'stop recording' when you finish.

If your audio software doesn't create an MP3 file automatically, you will need to do this manually; you could use iTunes software (which works on Mac and Windows) to do this. Once your file is converted to MP3, you can then upload it to your website or podcast directory (such as LibSyn[176] or Audioblog[177]) where your audience awaits.

Videoblogging

Videoblogs, or vlogs, which first appeared around 2000, have become much more popular in the last four or five years. The Indian Ocean tsunami in December 2004 was perhaps the first time that the mass availability of quality mobile video recording equipment and the occurrence of a huge natural disaster came together. There is no doubt about the power and immediacy of the live video format: BBC News commented on how the impact of these amateur accounts of the event eclipsed that of professional reporters and journalists[178].

As with podcasting, many 'traditional' written blogs include video clips too, although some blogs are entirely video-based[179]. Vlogs really can be created by anyone who has a PC and a webcam, mobile phone or digital camera or recorder to make the video with. You can host videos on your own blog if you're using software such

---

[176] http://www.libsyn.com

[177] http://www.audioblog.com/

[178] http://news.bbc.co.uk/1/hi/technology/4173787.stm

[179] For example http://trapperlosmd.blogspot.com/The Diary of Surgeon in a Warzone.

as Blogger[180] or Wordpress[181], or you can upload them to a dedicated video hosting site such as Youtube[182], one of the many alternatives, such as Bliptv.com[183], Viddler.com[184] or Vimeo.com[185], as well as to sites like Facebook, Flickr or MySpace. Whilst Youtube is the most well-known and well-used video-hosting website, it's worth bearing in mind that, with over ten hours of new content posted every minute[186], it's unlikely that your videos will be found unless someone is specifically looking for them.

But why might you want to enter into the world of vlogging? You could create a short video of yourself demonstrating your skills (for example, presenting, public speaking, training, facilitating or teaching) or a video résumé or CV. Whilst video CVs are still very much in their infancy, websites dedicated to hosting them are appearing[187]. Whether or not they will become mainstream is a different kettle of fish; it has been suggested that video CVs will stay on the margins because they reveal instantly a great deal of information that isn't necessarily available in a CV and which, legally, should not form part of the recruitment decision, such as age and ethnicity.

Don't let this put you off, however. If you're thinking about using a video CV, make sure it's well planned and well created. Whatever you do, avoid the example set by Aleksey Vayner, which we mentioned in Chapter 2.

---

180 https://www.blogger.com/start
181 http://wordpress.com/
182 http://www.youtube.com/
183 http://www.blip.tv/
184 http://www.viddler.com/
185 http://www.vimeo.com/
186 http://www.youtube.com/t/fact_sheet
187 E.g. http://www.meetyournewemployee.com

Top Tips for creating a professional video CV

1. First and foremost, a video CV is not a video of your CV! It's a short promotional video where you talk about yourself, your work experience and your major achievements.
2. Plan what you are going to say; write a tight one minute script covering the key points of your CV which you want to get across to your potential employer, then edit it down into bullet points. If possible, tailor your video résumé to fit the type of industry and job you want to apply for.
3. Make sure your surroundings are clean, uncluttered and quiet (no laundry drying on the radiator behind you, and you've switched off your mobile, for example).
4. Dress as you would dress for a face-to-face interview – usually smart business-wear.
5. Smile! Imagine you're talking to a real person, not the camera.
6. Don't read your script to the camera, instead use the bullet points to help prompt you and keep it sounding fresh and natural rather than overly rehearsed.
7. That said, you should practice what you're going to say; sometimes what you write sounds unnatural or affected when said out loud.
8. Ideally, aim to speak for about a minute, certainly no longer than that.
9. Speak clearly and confidently.
10. Make sure you introduce yourself, and include a polite sign-off including how you can be contacted.

11. Get a good friend or colleague to watch it and give you unbiased feedback.
12. Record yourself two or three times, and pick the best one.

If you're not sure whether an employer would be interested in watching a video résumé, 2007 research by American recruitment and career intelligence website Vault.com[188] suggested that 89% of employers would watch a video résumé if they were sent one, but only 17% have actually seen one. Additionally, employers surveyed said they would value a video résumé over and above a paper CV or application form because of their ability to assess the candidate's demeanour, presentation and speaking manner.

Don't forget that a video CV is only one step in the recruitment process, and that if you get over the first hurdle you can expect at least one face-to-face interview or request to attend an assessment centre.

We think video CVs are almost always likely to be used by students, freelancers wanting to return to full-time employment or those who are unemployed, and this may be another reason why they have been slow taking off. It's worth bearing in mind that you may therefore find yourself being labelled in a way that may not be helpful to your long-term career development. Finally, if you're already employed, you probably shouldn't risk your video CV being seen by your current employer!

---

188 http://www.vault.com/wps/portal/usa/!ut/p/c5/hVHLDoJADPwWv6AFZMHj6iqgsLqACnshENFoVEwkRPl64agGaNPTdGb6AAlN3tPqfErLc3FPrxCBJAlRJjwwbBXXY4uiYwprYXoOEkeBPUQ4ToKL-fDeZeTWsyq81AKfTLx52BQTNefZ5rDzt1PKwjJ7LRvNuFNTEL3HUdjGL1toDB0MuKcR3dVcZXBe-d3xz29x7AiKv_wvB7pTe3HBlH683b4H9_QBfUMFbhe3HJYgT9ciaz_IlAZpdB6lWSmE2ILHrVq5xJ_78yPLUzr6AEJIYxU!/dl3/d3/L3dJVkkvd0xNQUJvQWtnQSEhLzRCbjR0V0F5SUlBIS82XzYxOU5TN0gyME80R0EwSThRR0Y4TUkwUU8xLzNfQ0dBSDQ3TDAwTzJWMDAyTjVTUTBVUzMwSDUvbDNFQks1NTIwMDAwNw!!/?WCM_GLOBAL_CONTEXT=/wps/wcm/connect/Vault_Content_Library/articles_site/articles/news/89_+of+employers+open+to+viewing+video+resumes_+vault+video+resume+survey

A Vault.com survey[189] shows that 44% of employers use social networking web sites to screen candidates and 39% of them have viewed a current employee's profile. So if you're a student or someone wanting to return to full-time employment after a break, you can turn this to your advantage by adding a well-presented video CV or vlog to your social networking profile.

The Dos and Don'ts of traditional networking

Although the internet is an incredibly powerful, if under-used, networking resource, you shouldn't assume that you can always rely on it to further your career or personal development goals, whatever they happen to be; at some point you'll have to come out from behind your mobile, Blackberry, PC or Mac screen and leave the familiar territory of your favourite social networking site to meet real people face-to-face.

Of course, if you're an extrovert, the thought of pitching up at a formal networking lunch and handing round your newly-minted business cards won't faze you at all. Neither will the thought that you'll need to find some speaking opportunities of your own. In fact you'll probably enjoy the additional attention. But we suspect that there are a fair number of you who are actually far more confident when stationed behind your armoury of email, text and blog than when you're meeting a potential business contact or employer personally.

As we explored in some depth in earlier chapters, there is a whole raft of psychological processes at work to do with impression formation and management, interaction and non-verbal communication and behaviour, as well as cognitive biases which influence how relationships develop, and whether they blossom into anything more than mere acquaintanceships. We'll touch on

189 http://www.vault.com/wps/portal/usa/!ut/p/c5/04_SB8K8xLLM9MSSzPy8xBz9CP0os3gzQ0u_YHMPIwN_E3dHA0-LQHc3C19Pg0B_Q6B8JLJ8oLGLgadBsJ-vsZmpj7GPIQHd4SD78OsHyRvgAI4G6PpRbHAMM9L388jPTdUvyI0wyAxIVwQA1MUVBA!!/dI3/d3/L2dJQSEvUUt3QS9ZQnZ3LzZfNjE5TlM3SDIwTzRHQTBJOFFHRjhNSTBRRDE!/

some of these again in the next few sections, where we'll take you through the basics of face-to-face networking, such as how to prepare yourself mentally and physically, top tips for connecting with people, and controlling nerves.

Practical networking – What (not) to wear and what (not) to say

We've said this before but it's so important that we'll say it again – first impressions really do matter. Human relationships are at the heart of all our lives; people spend a huge amount of time thinking about other people that they've just met or just heard about (in real life, as well as on the TV, radio and internet), forming and reforming opinions about those they already know. The main reason for creating impressions of other people is to understand and predict their behaviour more effectively; this in turn allows us to respond in ways which will maximise our chances of achieving our goals, whatever they happen to be.

You already know that it's important to dress the part, so we won't dwell on that point again, especially since there is plenty of good advice already available. But as well as your physical appearance, you need to think about your 'presence', and whether your natural personality type is going to help or hinder your chances of achieving your networking goals. As we discussed earlier, psychological research[190] suggests that we attend to specific pieces of information about a person when we're forming a first impression; in particular, whether you're perceived as being 'warm' or 'cold' affects whether you make a favourable or unfavourable impression. The implication of this is that you need to appear confident, warm and friendly, even if this is not your natural way of being. This is made even more important by the existence of what psychologists have called 'the primacy effect', which is that people naturally seem to pay more attention to information which is presented first (primacy) and pay less attention to the information

[190] Asch, S.E. (1946). Forming impressions of personality. *Journal of Abnormal and Social Psychology, 41,* 258-90.

they find out later, especially when the earlier information is negative.[191] So whilst we wouldn't say that it's impossible to change a bad first impression, it is likely to be an uphill battle. Far better to start as you mean to go on. It might be worth remembering that if you're going to a group networking event, there are bound to be others there who feel nervous and apprehensive too.

Ten Top Tips to help you make a good impression

1. Take the bull by the horns and be the first to start up the conversation. Simple questions, like asking someone where they've come from, or why they decided to attend this event are a good way to start connecting.
2. Whatever you do, try to avoid starting with a complaint or something negative, since, even if you're just making small-talk about the weather or the traffic, it's very easy to be labelled as a negative person. No-one likes a whinger!
3. If the networking event features a speaker, you could ask what they already know of the speaker or the topic.
4. Remembering a person's name makes them feel important, so when you're introduced to other people, make an effort to remember. One way of doing this is to use their name immediately in your response 'Hi Jonathan, good to meet you too', since this helps to reinforce it.
5. Avoid sensitive subjects. Just as you would at any other social occasion, avoid topics like religion and politics.

---

[191] Fiske, S.T. (1980). Attention and weight on person perception. *Journal of Personality and Social Psychology, 38,* 889-906; Luchins, A.S. (1957). Primacy-recency in impression formation. In C. Howland (Ed.) *The Order of Presentation of Persuasion*. New Haven, CT: Yale University Press.

6. Be curious about the other people in the room. Ask open questions (starting with who, what, when, how).
7. Conversations can appear very one-sided if all you do is ask questions and give nothing away about yourself. So try to link what they have said to your own stories.
8. Prepare your 'elevator pitch' in advance (see Chapter 2 for further information), so that when you get asked what you do or why you are here, you can give a succinct and compelling response.
9. 'Fake it till you make it' is frequently used in coaching circles to inform people of the importance of their physiology to how they feel – you can role-play being a confident networker long enough for this to become a reality. So if you're lacking confidence, stand tall, keep your shoulders back, take a few deep breaths and smile!
10. Remember that others will be feeling pretty nervous too, even if they appear very confident.

How to build positive relationships

Psychology professor Shelley Gable and colleague's research[192] suggests that the most effective way to develop and maintain good relationships is through what is called 'active constructive responding'. In other words, when the person you are talking to tells you something positive, you respond by also displaying positive emotion and by asking them to elaborate.

So, for instance, if you ask someone at a networking event or conference how they came to be here and they reply they needed to find out about e-marketing trends because they'd just been

[192] Gable, S,L., Impett, E.A., Reis, H.T. & Ascher, E.R. (2004). What do you do when things go right? The intrapersonal and interpersonal benefits of sharing positive events. Journal of personality and Social Psychology, 87(2), 228-245.

promoted to a new role in their organisation, you could use that opportunity to respond enthusiastically with something like 'congratulations, do tell me more!', thereby getting them to replay the positive event and capitalise on it. According to Professor Gable, active constructive responding conveys understanding, validation and caring, and is more important to the development of social relationships than how you respond to negative events. So, be on the look-out for opportunities to respond in an active constructive way; it will help you appear interested, and keep the conversation positive and inspiring.

Managing your time well

When there are lots of people at a networking event, plan and manage your time carefully. The danger is that you'll hook up with one or two people that you get on with very well, and talk to them all evening rather than move on and meet new people. Before you know it, the event will be over and you may have missed a good opportunity.

So if you can, get hold of a list of attendees – some networking events distribute one beforehand, some hand them out at the event, whereas others don't do it at all. If you're lucky enough to be given a list, scan it to see who you would like to meet – you may be able to tell a little bit about the person from their job title and organisation. This will give you an objective for the event, a goal to aim for, as well as a starting point for a conversation. In terms of building networking confidence and resilience, having a goal to achieve also helps to relieve your anxiety, since your attention will be diverted away from how you feel.

At the same time, don't make the mistake of dismissing everyone else who is there just because their job title or organisation seems irrelevant to you – after all their partner, colleague or neighbour may be just the person that you do need to meet.

Ten Great Networking Questions

1. How did you come to be involved in.... [industry/sector/ job]?
2. What do you like best about what you do?
3. And if you could change one thing about your role, what would it be?
4. What do you see are the main trends in....?
5. How would you describe the ideal [employee/customer/ supplier] for your organisation?
6. What advice would you give someone just starting up in.... [this business/profession/sector]?
7. What are the most important qualities you need to succeed in... [this job/ profession]?
8. Who do you know who could give me some further insight into....?
9. Who do you recommend I contact about......?
10. Where else do you normally network?

Finishing on a high note

Don't forget that you have clear networking goals (see Chapter 2 for a reminder) and in order to achieve them, you will need to share your objectives with other people. So you will need to ask for what you want, in a way which enables them to help you. Trying using one or more of the 'Ten Great Networking Questions' above to break the ice, find out more about the person you're talking to and to gauge whether they might be able to help you further in your professional, business or career quest.

Inevitably at some point during the networking session, you will need to end a conversation and move on. Perhaps the person you're speaking to cannot help you (and you cannot help them), or you desperately need to talk to someone else before they leave. As you should never leave someone standing on their own at a networking event, one of the best ways of moving on is to introduce them to someone else.

Following up

After a face-to-face networking event, always acknowledge the people you met, either by email, or through your social network, and if you promised to send them any information, make sure you do. Your email or message needs to be brief, mention when and where you met, and if appropriate, thank them for their advice or make a suggestion to meet, or to talk on the phone. We also advise that you 'google' the people you meet as soon as possible, to find out as much information about them, what they do and who they work for.

Additionally, make sure you follow up any leads that you have been given, since the longer you leave it, the less likely it is that you will.

Maintaining a positive mindset

I have not failed. I've just found 10,000 ways that won't work.
Thomas A. Edison

Sometimes your networking plans may not run as smoothly as you would like; perhaps you don't make any worthwhile connections at all or worse, when you do pluck up the courage to ask someone for something, you get an instant rejection. This can be hard, especially if you're new to the networking scene. Psychologist and researcher Carol Dweck[193] suggests that people with a fixed mindset find knock-backs of this kind particularly difficult; they label themselves as failures and vow never to repeat the experience. According to Dweck, people with a growth mindset believe that they can learn how to do things differently such that next time, they're more likely to be successful. There is increasing evidence from the field of neuroscience which suggests that connections between information-carrying neurons in the brain continue to grow as we learn new things – in other words, the brain actually increases in

[193] Dweck, C. (2006). *Mindset: The new psychology of success*. New York, NY US: Random House

density. Taxi-drivers, for example, have a denser hippocampus (the area in the brain which deals with 3D space) than do non-taxi-drivers. So, where does this leave you, the fledgling networker? Well, our advice would be to always keep rejection in perspective (for more advice on how to handle set-backs, see Chapter 6). Maybe the person you asked really cannot help you, or cannot help you at this time. Perhaps if you ask them again later or in a few weeks they might say yes. Start creating a growth mindset by thinking about whether you can do anything differently to be more effective next time – perhaps your request could be clearer, or could be made mutually beneficial.

6

Developing and implementing your personal networking strategy

In the previous five chapters we've covered everything about online networking, from the basics of what it is and which networks to join, to why it's important for your career, plus the practical Dos and Don'ts. Alongside this we've introduced the latest psychology research and how this can help you understand and make the most of your online experience. We want you to be able to approach e-networking confidently and effectively, combining best practice from 'traditional' offline networking with the possibilities and potentials for broader and more numerous business relationships that the internet offers.

In Chapter 2 we introduced you to the subject of goal-setting. If you haven't revisited your online networking goals since then, now is a good time to do so. Reflect on what it is that you want to achieve through e-networking. Spell out your goal in as much detail as possible, using the SMART approach.

Once you're happy with your goal, you can start to think about how you're going to achieve it, and what all the smaller steps are along the route. One way of looking at this is to think of your goal as the destination, and your strategy as the journey. Say you want to go from London to Brighton – would you take the train (and if so, first class? economy? through train or slow train?), or go by coach, car, or even bike? The method you choose has implications for time, effort and cost, all of which are also important considerations for your online networking strategy.

No time on your hands?

Like the slow train or through train to Brighton, you can adopt different approaches to your networking strategy; usually it's a trade-off between the amount of time and effort required, and what it'll cost you. For instance, you can stick to using the free LinkedIn and Ecademy services and build up your network over time, or you can opt to pay for their additional services (see LinkedIn and Ecademy's websites for current charges) and get a bit of a head-start.

That said, it's perfectly possible to build a pretty healthy network of connections through these sites without paying a penny, so if you're on a budget our advice is to start with the free services and think about upgrading once you begin to realise some tangible returns. These don't have to be monetary; perhaps getting contacts who are clearly interested in developing a business relationship with you, or actually progressing to face-to-face meetings could be your initial goal. After all, there are hundreds of thousands of successful business people using these websites every day, and a great number use them for free.

Quantity or Quality?

As we mentioned in Chapter 2, you can also build up a substantial network using Twitter; in fact, it's much easier and quicker to build up a large following in Twitter than to make contacts in LinkedIn. But you have to bear in mind that it's also much less easy to substantiate the calibre of your Twitter contacts without additional online evidence, such as a website, blog or credible profile on a business or social network site. Social network researchers from Hewlett Packard have suggested that the cost (in time and effort) associated with maintaining relationships is such that the actual number of people that Twitter users frequently interact with is in reality far smaller than their number of followers[194]; in other words,

[194] Huberman, B., Romero, D, & Wu, F. (2009). Social networks that matter: Twitter under the

their 'real' friends are a small subset. Nevertheless, don't forget the power of the weak tie, which we discussed in Chapter 1.

On the other hand, when someone is recommended to you, via LinkedIn for instance, you need have less concern about their credentials, merely because of the fact that they have been recommended by one of your trusted contacts. Twitter doesn't have this kind of in-built trust mechanism. Ecademy is neither one thing nor the other – of course there are many credible and successful people who use Ecademy very effectively to make real and long-lasting business relationships which are mutually beneficial, but equally there are others who are just out to make a quick buck and give you nothing in return. So you do need to be a bit network savvy! Remember, all the psychology research points to the rapid development of online relationships, but you should ultimately test their value through phone calls or face-to-face meetings if possible.

Comparison of main network characteristics

	Cost	Size of your network	Speed of network growth	Level of trust in contacts
LinkedIn	Free, with optional paid-for services	Relatively small	Relatively slow	Very high
Ecademy	Free, with optional paid-for services	Relatively large	Relatively fast	Med-low
Twitter	Free	Very large	Fastest	Low
Facebook	Free,with optional paid-for applications	Very large	Faster	Low

microscope. *First Monday, 14 (1).*

Maintaining your e-network relationships

There really is no such thing as a free lunch! Like all relationships, those you create on social networks need to be looked after. Give and take forms a crucial part in all social and economic transactions[195], and those on the internet really are no different. This means that you should set aside some time on a regular basis to actively cultivate new online relationships and nurture existing ones. Mark the time out in your diary so that it does get done.

How to find new contacts:

The internet has facilitated your ability to make new contacts literally at the touch of a button. The skill comes in knowing where to look. Here are a few ideas to start you off:

- Join new groups and start contributing to the conversation. Be helpful; add links to information that will be useful to other group members. In Ecademy you can search through the profiles and CVs of other club members; this will give you a good insight into what people have done and what they're current interests are. Joining groups and clubs in your field of expertise is a good way of keep up to date with the current issues and opinions.
- Use the LinkedIn Answers function (see Chapter 3), either to ask your own questions or provide answers to others'. Although this application is not officially for the purpose of making new contacts, there is nothing to stop you embarking on conversations with other LinkedIn users, then asking them to join your network.

And if you have any spare time in your busy schedule, random searching and following on Twitter can lead to all sort of interesting connections. For instance, do a search in Twitter on your profession, or using some keywords from your field of expertise, and just see what comes up. Follow any interesting leads. Look at the groups

[195] Fehr, E & Gachter, S. (2000). Fairness and retaliation: The economics of reciprocity. *Journal of Economic Perspectives, 14 (3),* 159-181.

that your LinkedIn contacts have joined, read the conversations and contribute if you can. Check out new groups on Facebook, join them and contribute to the discussion. You never know who you might meet this way.

How to nurture existing contacts:

- Keep a look out for news and information, business developments, interesting websites, contracts and tips which might be useful to the people in your network. Pass them on by phone or email as soon as you can.
- Keep up to date with what your contacts are currently doing. Set aside an hour a week to review your lists of LinkedIn contacts and Facebook friends and read their updates. Make time to ring them or email them on a regular basis.
- Make use of e-cards – you can send them on birthdays (making use of the email reminders you get from sites like Plaxo for example), or to mark promotions or other career and life successes.
- Keep your contacts up to date with what you're currently working on. This can be done quite easily in LinkedIn by making updates to your profile, job title or headline, which will then be reported on the regular LinkedIn Network Update emails.

Our advice is: don't wait for 'the right time' to make contact – just call on the spur of the moment to say hello and ask how things are going.

Use your time effectively. If you're waiting (for a plane, taxi or even for a large report to print), use the time to connect with people by phone, text, email or IM.

Strategy: turning your networking goal into reality

OK, so now we get into the real meat of this chapter: how to turn your networking goal(s) into reality. Just to start you thinking creatively about all the different ways you can use online networking, we're going to use some examples, and suggest ways in which you might develop an effective strategy.

Firstly if you think Facebook and Twitter are just about keeping up with your friends and family then you're missing out on a potential goldmine. You need to change your mindset about the power of online networking.

How social networking can give you and your business a competitive edge

According to Sylvia Cambié and Yang-May Ooi, experts in international communications and social media and co-authors of *International communications strategy: Developments in cross-cultural communications, PR and social media*[196], social networking and other social media are an extension of what you would normally do to develop your business and your brand in the real world. Whilst Cambié and Ooi acknowledge that social media are not suitable for everyone or every business, they suggest that it is possible to derive significant business benefits from using social networking if:

- You are passionate about your business, industry or area of expertise
- You know who your customers and clients are and want to engage with them
- You enjoy engaging with people anyway
- You value networking and take care to develop business and personal relationships

Take US business consultant and International Coach Federation certified coach, Kathryn Britton, director of Theano Coaching[197]. Britton is passionate about helping her clients make a positive difference to the world, and like most successful coaches, the vast

---

[196] Cambié, S & Ooi, YM. (2009). International communications strategy: Developments in cross-cultural communications, PR, and social media. London, Kogan Page, pp112-113.
[197] http://theano-coaching.com/index.html

majority of her work comes from referrals. Since she's a natural networker, LinkedIn has become an essential business-generating tool for her. Apart from collecting recommendations (she has almost 10% from the 636 connections in her network), she distributes a regular newsletter. Britton says, *'My newsletter is a way to touch people in a helpful way once a month, reminding them of what I can do for them if they need a coach or consultant. I get emails back from people who've found the information useful. Sometimes I touch a nerve. Now I'm beginning to see value from LinkedIn beyond the roll-o-dex function.'*

So assuming you're onboard with the idea that internet-based networking can help you achieve your business goals, let's dive right in!

Finding a new job

If your goal is to find a job, typical approaches include reading the vacancies section of local newspapers, looking at job websites such as Monster[198], Gumtree[199] and Jobsearch[200], and sending a CV on spec to companies that you want to work for. In terms of e-networking strategies, you also have several different options, which are more likely to be successful because you'll be making use of your personal connections.

How to use LinkedIn's Advanced Job Search

1. If you know what sort of job you're looking for, LinkedIn's Advanced Job Search function can help you track it down. Simply click on the Jobs button on the top menu and then click on the Advanced Job Search tab. From here you can search for jobs by:

    - job title or keyword (anything and everything from account managers to web developers)

[198] http://www.monster.co.uk/ and http://jobsearch.monster.com/
[199] http://www.gumtree.com/jobs
[200] http://www.jobsearch.com

- job function
- company
- industry
- location (any country in the world, any county in the UK, or within a specified radius from a specified postcode)
- experience level
- most recent job adverts posted.

We recommend that you start with a wide search and narrow it down, to ensure that you don't miss out any opportunities.

2. Click 'search' to see a full listing of those vacancies which match your criteria.

3. There are several benefits to using LinkedIn's jobsearch function. Firstly you can find out the name of the member of staff who posted the job in LinkedIn, and get a link to their profile. Secondly if the person is in your network already, you get to see whether they're a first, second or third level connection. This means that you then have the option of getting a referral (sometimes called an Introduction in LinkedIn jargon) to them (see below); we highly recommend doing this if you have time. Thirdly, when you click on a job you're interested in, you get to see if anyone in your network already works at that company and may potentially provide you with some assistance.

   Click on the individual job(s) that you're interested in. If you don't have time to get introduced to the person concerned, you should proceed to apply there and then. Click on the Apply Now button the right hand side of the screen. Then you'll be taken to a job application screen (which may be a generic one or a company-specific one). Here you'll need to write your covering letter (or cut and paste one from Word if you have one already prepared).

4. Scroll down the page to add your contact information.

5. Finally upload a copy of your CV.

6. The last step is to click on 'Next' to review your application before clicking on 'Submit Application'.

Although LinkedIn's job search function doesn't yet feature as many vacancies as some of the other commercial recruitment websites, if your particular search doesn't retrieve any relevant jobs on LinkedIn itself, it will then continue the search for you on the web anyway. It does this using 'Simply Hired', a vertical job search engine that aggregates vacancy information from right across the web, using listings on job boards, company pages, classified adverts and other recruitment websites such as Monster, Reed and Job Search. And if you enable the JobInsider toolbar (see above), by clicking on the LinkedIn logo next to the company name in Simply Hired, you can still track down any existing LinkedIn contacts who can help you make connections there. So you'll rarely come back from a LinkedIn job search empty-handed.

Although it may see a little obvious, we're going to say it anyway. When you submit your CV via LinkedIn, in all probability the hiring manager will check out your LinkedIn profile. This means that your profile and your CV have to be consistent. So there's no point applying for a job as a senior marketing manager if it's evident from your LinkedIn profile that you don't have any previous experience of or interest in the marketing world. On the other hand, it can add an enormous amount of kudos and credibility to your application if you've worked in marketing before, and you also have recommendations from people for the work you have done in this field.

How to Use LinkedIn's Company Search

The company search function on LinkedIn is also a useful way to find current vacancies. If you know which company you're interested in, click on 'Companies' on the menu at the top of the home page, type in the company name and click 'search companies'. You'll get a page of useful information about the company, including a list of your first and second contacts who work there (if there are any), a list current and former employees, promotions, new recruits, as well as some key statistics about the company, such as common job titles, average age, percentage male/female, stock market indices (if relevant), and recent news coverage. Your first level contacts may be able to provide you with some useful inside information about the job being advertised, and may also be able to introduce you to one of the hiring team.

If you don't know exactly which company you're looking for and want to carry out a broad search, then click on 'show more', about half way down the page. You will then have the option to search by size of company, type of industry as well as by location, plus you can limit your search to only those companies you are linked to at one or two levels, and by those which are currently hiring. Alongside the list of companies which match your search criteria will be shown the number of current advertised vacancies; if you click on this you will be presented with a list of jobs, showing location, date and the company representative who posted the vacancy. If you click on the company name instead, you will be taken to the page of company information, as mentioned above.

How to make your networking profile more attractive

So you can make LinkedIn work harder on your behalf by making your profile as visible and appealing as possible. Here are some tips:

Seven ways to enhance your LinkedIn networking profile

1. Get recommendations. As we suggested in Chapter 2 above, getting some endorsements in LinkedIn can add enormous value to your profile. However, we firmly believe that you can overdo recommendations. It's quality not quantity that counts. So get a variety of recommendations, for instance from several high profile customers, or from a range of previous managers and colleagues, but don't go overboard. Busy HR and recruiting professionals are unlikely to have the time to read dozens of recommendations, so choose a few of the best ones to

show on your LinkedIn profile. Always ask the people you have worked with for recommendations, but use your judgement before automatically showing them on your profile (you have the option to keep them hidden, see Chapter 2 above).

2. Make sure your LinkedIn profile is up-to-date, and reflects all the key roles that you have undertaken. Highlight your accomplishments, but be factual. As we suggested in Chapter 2, choose your words carefully and avoid technical jargon and acronyms (unless this is unavoidable in your field of work). Make sure you use relevant keywords that are likely to come up in a hiring manager's search.

3. Link to all your alumni and previous colleagues. Check the LinkedIn Groups directory to see whether your previous college, university or employer has an alumni group; if so, join it. As suggested in Chapter 3 above, you can search the members list of your alumni group for old classmates, tutors or colleagues that you would like to reconnect with.

4. Look at the profiles of your current connections, and when you find a particularly appealing one, work out what they do effectively and apply the technique to your own profile.

5. Remember that everything you write on your social network profile should enhance your personal brand positioning, or be relevant to your 'story' (see Chapter 2). When you create your LinkedIn profile, think about what you'd write in a traditional CV: don't list all the jobs you have ever done if they're not relevant to your current job search, don't add to your overall 'story', or help to explain how and why you are who you are. So you'll need to use your judgement here.

6. Revisit your profile(s) at a later date. The passage of time is a great way to gain the objectivity needed to edit what you've written and improve on it (and spot any typos that

you previously didn't notice). So, make sure you go back to your profile and read what you wrote about yourself a few days or weeks before: how does it come across? What is your immediate impression? What does it say about you? Does it reflect who you really are? If you have trouble doing this, ask a trusted friend or colleague for their feedback.

7. Don't forget that you can also enhance your reputation and make your profile more appealing by using the LinkedIn 'Answers' function. As we suggested in Chapter 3, this is an ideal way to showcase the expertise and experience you have in your subject and your industry. Plus if your Twitter and Facebook profiles and activities support your LinkedIn profile, this strengthens your personal brand too.

Other ways to search for that dream job using LinkedIn

Use LinkedIn's advanced Search option to find the top five or six companies that you are most interested in working for.

Again you will get a list of information including who in your current network is connected to these companies and at what level (first, second, third). You can ask them to introduce you to someone at that company. Make sure you have your pitch ready – in other words, you know what you are looking for and you can clearly spell out what you have to offer them. If in doubt, imagine you're a potential Apprentice in Sir Alan Sugar's boardroom and answer the question: 'Why should I hire you?'

Don't forget that even if no-one in your network currently works for the companies you're interested in, they may have done in the past. If that's the case, they may be able and willing to provide you with valuable inside information, tips or contacts which could prove useful in your job search.

An inside job?

LinkedIn has a unique function called JobInsider which you use in conjunction with other online job search sites (such as Monster, Craigslist and Gumtree[201],) to show the LinkedIn connections you already have to the companies which are advertising the jobs. JobInsider works by simply analysing the details of the job posting, and using the employer name to trigger any existing connections that you have in LinkedIn.

To enable JobInsider, go to the LinkedIn home page, scroll down to the bottom of the page, and click on JobInsider which is in the Tools section. From here you simply download the JobInsider toolbar by clicking on the JobInsider for Internet Explorer or Firefox links. Then when you go to Monster, or Craigslist (or a number of other external job search websites), enable the JobInsider function by clicking on the LinkedIn icon on the top right hand side of the page and finding JobInsider on the menu. A new pane will appear on the left hand side of your screen. Then, when you find a job on Monster you are interested in, any connections you already have at that particular company will be flagged up in the JobInsider pane. You can scroll through these to find mutual connections, and choose the most promising connection you have.

The beauty of this system is, of course, that you can use your contacts inside the company to get you introduced to the relevant HR or hiring manager within the hiring company. Your LinkedIn contact might even be able to put in a good word for you. As ever in the job market, 'it's who you know, not what you know' that counts, so using JobInsider has got to be a good thing for you.

Do bear in mind though that JobInsider isn't 100% fool-proof. For one thing, it relies on the hiring company being named in the job ad, and as you know, a significant number of jobs are actually advertised indirectly through agencies, without the hiring company being revealed. But if you want to increase the chances of having a connection to someone inside the hiring company, then you do need to make sure that you continue to grow your network and add

[201] www.monster.co.uk, www.craigslist.co.uk, www.gumtree.com

new connections on a regular basis.

Now that we have explored some different strategies for finding a job based on using LinkedIn, let's look at how you could use Facebook, and the different things you could do with it.

How to find a job using Facebook

Unlike LinkedIn, Facebook is a social network rather than a business network (although this is changing as companies create their own Facebook pages), but don't let that put you off using it to find a job. Facebook is still an excellent medium to use to enhance your chances of getting that dream role, and it's worth investing some time thinking about how you can take advantage of its functionality to tap into some of the millions of worldwide users. An increasing number of influential business people are using Facebook for their own social networking purposes, so if you use it regularly, the chances are that you might end up joining the same groups. Even if you don't use Facebook actively to find a job, you should be aware that an increasing number of employers are looking up the profiles of potential hires before asking them to interview, so you need to make sure that your profile is as attractive as possible.

Preparation:

1. Most importantly make sure your profile page 'matches' the job you are looking for. So if you're looking for a job in a creative or media field, your profile, photos and groups should showcase your creativity and media savvy.

   For instance, if your degree is in marketing and you're looking for a job in that field, make sure your profile is an example of good marketing, and make sure you have joined and contributed to some groups which are related to marketing and which support your 'brand'.

   If you're looking for a job in fashion journalism, and your Facebook groups are related to rugby, CAMRA and haute cuisine rather than news media, design and haut couture, and you have nothing on your Facebook profile which sells your passion for fashion, then prospective employers are unlikely to be convinced. You need to tell a compelling story. If you are lucky enough to get an interview, you'll have to work a whole lot harder to convince them that you're a catwalk-savvy journo rather than a beer-swilling Twickenham groupie.

2. Be clear about what you are looking for. The chances of meeting a newspaper or magazine editor looking for a fashion journalist or writer on your first attempt at networking are pretty limited. So not only should you be prepared for 'failure' (see below for some more information on building your networking resilience) but you should be clear about exactly what you want from the people you do meet.

   After all, if the 'six degrees of separation' theory is true, then you're never very far away from a person who could help you make your career dream a reality. Don't forget that in LinkedIn you can do a quick check on how many people are in your second and third level networks by clicking on the 'Network Statistics' tab from the left hand menu. In my network I have over 100 first level contacts, over 12,700 second level contacts and over 1.2 *million* third level contacts. And since Facebook networks are generally larger than LinkedIn networks, you'll have even more contacts in Facebook. So think about what you want from the people you meet in Facebook groups. Spend some time honing your Elevator Pitch – your 30-second 'personal commercial' about you, what you have to offer and why someone else might be interested in it. As we have already mentioned in Chapter 3, e-networking relationships work best when they are reciprocal, so think about what you could also offer the people that you meet online.

Top Tips for asking for help

- Be specific, ask for advice, and use open:

  I'm looking for a job [in fashion journalism]. Who do you know who has connections in the fashion industry or the media who could [give me some advice/ act as a mentor etc]?

  I'm looking for a job in [XYZ company / industry / sector] or I'm looking for a job as a [role]. Who do you know who could give me some advice?

- Avoid closed questions:

  I'm looking for a job. Do you know anyone I can talk to?

  Likely response: rather than clarifying your request, the person you're asking may take the easy route and just say 'no'.

- Finally, don't make demands and don't ask for information which will compromise them.

Action:

Join appropriate Facebook groups, e.g. those related to journalism, fashion, design, and anything else which supports your endeavour. Make friends with other group members, help them if you can, and check them out on LinkedIn (or Ecademy) as well. Most people who are serious about their work or their industry will have a profile in one (or both) of these networks too. Remember the reciprocity rule: that there needs to be give and take for a healthy relationship to flourish.

Join in the Group's conversation about issues related to your industry or job, or start the conversation if there isn't one already (see our tips above about using LinkedIn Answers).

Don't be put off when you seem to get to a dead end. Imagine the job you are looking for is in the centre of a vast maze. The maze has a number of different entrances, and routes to the centre, but these are not clear at the start – they're hidden until you start exploring them. You're likely to end up down some blind alleys along the way, in which case just start again.

How to be innovative with your Facebook job search

A much more pro-active, and innovative, approach is to use Facebook adverts yourself to target the company that you want to work for. This requires a bit of input, in preparing the job advert, and you will have to pay for the ad, although you can set a budget in Facebook to ensure you don't run up a large bill.

Case Study – Using Facebook ads to make employers track you down

This method of searching for a job has been tried and tested in an experiment carried out by Willy Franzen, a young graduate of Cornell University, USA. Franzen's experience of job search after he left college was so frustrating that he set up a website, One Day One Job[202] to help fellow graduates along the way.

He recruited five website readers to participate in the experiment. With Franzen's help and guidance, they each created a simple Facebook advertising campaign for themselves, targeted at specific companies, industries or locations. The adverts read something like:

Title: I want to work for [company]/ in [industry]
Photo:
Content: *Hi, I'm [name]. I recently graduated from [university] with a degree in [subject]. My dream is to work for*

[202] www.onedayonejob.com

[company]/in [industry]. Can you help? Click here [insert link] to see my CV.

The results were as follows:

	Ad views	*Clicks*	*Cost*	*Result*
Laura Pilkington	2288	44	$9.24	Made new contacts, opened up new conversations about possible jobs
Alex Payne	622	20	n/a	Found out about new opportunities and received new information about jobs
Baker Barnett	35315	76	$26.93	Received suggestions about where to apply for jobs
Michael West	2588	32	$5.12	Informal interview at targeted company
Katelyn Hill	n/a	685	n/a	Official interview received advice about getting a job with targeted company

Although none of these graduates immediately got a job as a result of their Facebook advert, they all got inside information about the jobs market, and it made them stand out as a candidate, which is crucial when the competition for jobs is tough.

If you want to stand out of the crowd, and be seen as a proactive job-hunter, this method is worth trying. For a step-by-step guide on how to do it, see www.onedayonejob.com[203].

A word of advice before you use a Facebook advert – make sure you have set your privacy settings correctly (see chapter 2 for more information), so that only trusted friends can view your Facebook profile.

Another goal, another strategy?

Say your goal is to have a book published, how might you use social networking to help you?

Traditional versus e-networking approaches

Opportunity: you haven't published a book before but you've got a very original idea and you want to find a company which would be interested in publishing it.

Traditional approach: write a proposal and maybe a first chapter to demonstrate your flair for writing and to tempt the prospective publisher into handing over a multi-million pound advance (we can all dream!). You might visit your local library to borrow, or buy, a copy of the annual Writers Yearbook[204]. You thumb through it, looking for the names of companies which publish book in this genre, be it business, fiction or whatever. You then proceed to mail them all a copy of your proposal and first chapter, and sit back and eagerly await a phone call or letter to say 'Yes we'd like to meet you to discuss publishing your book'.

Unfortunately, the vast majority of book proposals and

[203] http://www.onedayonejob.com/blog/use-facebook-ads-to-make-employers-hunt-you-down/

[204] Mosse, K (2008). Writers' and artists' yearbook 2009: A directory for writers, artists, playwrights, designers, illustrators and photographers. London .A&C Black Publishers Ltd.

unsolicited manuscripts get turned down, not once or twice but three times or more. You won't even get as far as meeting anyone from the publishing company to make a pitch in person, and to persuade them of the brilliance of your book idea. Even if they're bestsellers-in-waiting, they end up getting binned, shredded or used as spare paper for the kids to draw on. Hmm, not a nice way for your dream to finish is it?

E-networking approach: What would that same goal look like if your strategy was to find a publisher via your online network? There are so many different possibilities, all of which are more likely to lead to success than the unsolicited manuscript method. Getting an introduction to someone via an existing LinkedIn connection instantly gives you more credibility, because you're being introduced by someone who knows you, and who is vouching for you (remember what we said in Chapter 4 about LinkedIn and trust?). So it's not like sending a random email to someone you've never met, or cold calling them. By having your LinkedIn, Ecademy, Facebook or Twitter connection act as a 'go between', effectively you're being represented by someone else who already has credibility and standing in the eyes of the person you want to impress, which of course is all in your favour! So providing you've done your homework and found a publishing house which is a good fit for your proposal, you're far more likely to be able to set up a meeting and pitch your idea to them in person than if you were to cold-call them.

Investigate the connections you already have on Linked In. Which ones have worked in publishing companies? Which ones have other connections in publishing? If they have, contact them and tell them about your goal. Ask them for their help to find a connection who you can talk to for specific advice.

Or, having already done your homework about the publishers who might be interested in your book idea, you can search LinkedIn using the Companies Search function, then see if any of your current connections have contacts in that specific publishing company, and whether they are second or third level contacts.

Network of 1st, second and third level contacts

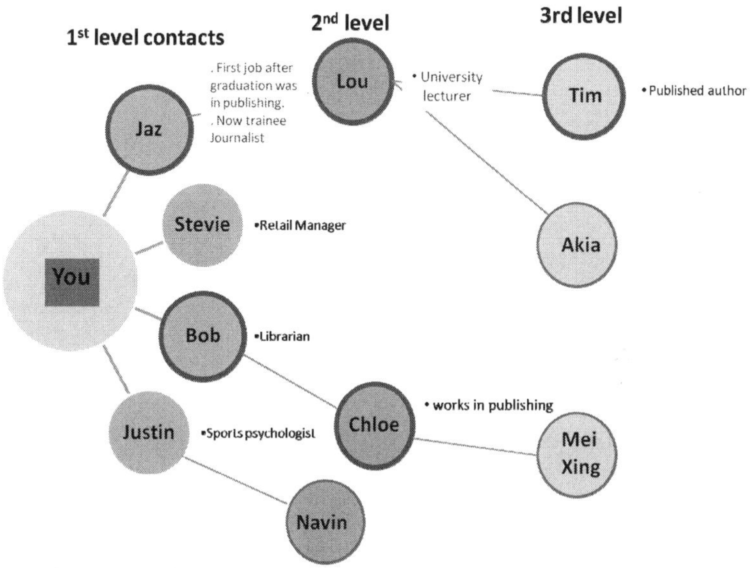

Unless you already work in the media or literary field or have a substantial LinkedIn network, it may be that none of your immediate, first level contacts will have worked in a publishing company before, so you will more than likely have to go through second and third level contacts. Don't be overly concerned about this, LinkedIn networks are very robust; we have known people get referred through networks to third level contacts very quickly.

Once you have found a potential contact, you'll need to ask your immediate connection to introduce you. You'll also need to have a ready-made pitch which explains what you have to offer, and why the publisher could benefit, so prepare a solid (but concise) pitch to introduce your idea in a persuasive and compelling fashion. Remember, as with all pitches, you do have to be prepared to explain concisely what you have to offer the other party, NOT what you want to gain from the transaction.

How to get an introduction to a second level connection in LinkedIn

1. Be prepared! Write down your concise and compelling pitch, which spells out what how the person you want to be connected to will benefit from being connected to you, as well as what you are offering. Don't give excuses as to why you want to be connected to them. And don't leave your request until it becomes urgent; other people work to different deadlines; what might be urgent for you may be far less important to them.

2. Be polite and be patient! You're relying on the goodwill of your 1st level contact to send your Introduction on to their contact, so be polite and be patient. Don't expect them to forward your Introduction straight away – remember whilst you may be logged into LinkedIn 24/7, some people log in only occasionally, and may not log in at all at weekends or on holiday. Don't pester! But if the Introduction goes unanswered for a couple of weeks, by all means follow up with a polite and friendly phone call.

3. Do a favour in return – reciprocity is the name of the game in social and business networking, so make sure you volunteer a way of giving back a benefit to your connection for the introduction they have made for you.

Say you want to be introduced to Chloe Carpenter, who is a second level connection to you through your contact Bob. Before you send a request to Bob for an introduction, read Chloe's LinkedIn profile page to make sure that she is happy to receive Introductions – some people on LinkedIn specifically say they are not accepting Introductions, perhaps if they are too busy at the time to deal with them. Make sure you stick to this, because there's nothing more likely to ruin a potentially strong business relationship than overstepping the mark at the start. You'll see in the middle right hand side of the page a flow chart which shows how you are connected to this person and whether they are second or third level contacts. Then at the top right hand side of their profile is a button marked 'Get Introduced through a connection'. Click on this link, and you will be taken to the Introductions page.

On the Introductions page, fill in the details of the person you want to meet (Chloe Carpenter), your email address and phone number, and select the right category of request from the drop down list (e.g. career opportunity, consulting offer, new venture, job enquiry, expertise or reference request, business deal of to get back in touch). Then you need to write a concise and compelling message to Chloe, followed by a message to Bob, asking him to make the Introduction on your behalf.

To Chloe Carpenter you might write something like:

Hello Chloe, I notice that your company has just launched a series of concise paperback guides for business managers on technology-related subjects. I have a proposal for a guide about managing virtual teams using new technologies which would fit very well alongside your existing titles. I would like to connect with you to share this information, and explore how this might be of benefit to you.

Kind regards
Alex Atkins

To Bob you might write something like:

Hi Bob, it was good to speak to you earlier today about my latest project. Here's the introduction I mentioned; I'd be really grateful if you could pass it on to Chloe Carpenter for me. Many thanks!

Alex

After writing a message to both Chloe and Bob, click the send button.

Possible reasons why a first-level contact might decline your request

Say you've just send off your carefully crafted message to Bob, asking him to forward your request for an Introduction to Chloe, but he comes back and says 'No'. What might his reasons be?

1. It may be that Chloe is a relatively new connection in Bob's network, and so he may not feel comfortable with passing an introduction on so soon.
2. Perhaps Chloe is a very old connection, and Bob has already passed on a great many introductions and thus he feels uncomfortable adding yet another one.
3. Maybe he knows Chloe very well and knows that she doesn't like receiving Introductions on LinkedIn.
4. Or maybe Bob volunteers that he thinks that Chloe would respond to a different type of approach, or a differently worded message. Either way, take whatever feedback he gives you gracefully, and work with it!

Even if you're disappointed when Bob turns down your request, don't take it personally. If there is something you can improve in your message to Chloe, he will be sure to tell you. It may be that Bob can give you a bit of insider information about how exactly to contact Chloe so as to maximise the chances of your proposal coming to fruition. But if he says that in his experience Chloe won't accept your LinkedIn Introduction, take this information as a Golden Tip and move on. Continue your search for other connections at this publishing house, or at another company which might equally well fit the bill.

And what if none of your connections have any second or third hand connections to Chloe Carpenter? Is there any other way of using LinkedIn to introduce yourself to her?

How to send LinkedIn InMail

An InMail is a private message on LinkedIn which allows you to contact or be contacted by another LinkedIn user directly, without going through a mutual connection and without knowing the recipient's email address. You can use the InMail application as a part of a premium account package. LinkedIn claims that InMail isn't free to prevent spammers from using it. At the time of writing (July 2009), the cost works out at about $10 per InMail.

Using InMail also protects the recipient's privacy, since their email address isn't revealed. If a LinkedIn member is happy for you to contact them via InMail (i.e. they've set their Contact Settings to be open to accept InMail), a 'Send InMail' link will be displayed in the top right corner of their profile page. If the person you want to connect to isn't in your network, you won't see their name or contact information until they've accepted your InMail.

Going back to our example goal of finding a book publisher, you could still contact Chloe Carpenter, even if you have no second or third hand connections, by using InMail. The obvious advantage of using InMail is speed: you can contact any member of LinkedIn (providing they are open to accepting InMail – which you can check by looking at the top RHS of their profile page) directly without having to find someone in your existing network who is connected to them. This might be a great benefit if you are in a rush to establish contact, but remember that old saying 'more haste less speed'; the obvious disadvantage is that, aside from the fact that you are both LinkedIn members, there is initially nothing else to connect you, so this approach is more like cold-calling.

Providing you've done your homework on your intended connection and you've written a polite and persuasive request, you have nothing to lose by trying a direct InMail. As with Introductions, be patient whilst you wait for a response. Although best practise would suggest that if you receive an InMail from another LinkedIn member you respond as quickly as possible, do remember that your intended connection might be in the middle of a crucial business deal, handling some other crisis, or they may be on holiday. Any of these reasons could explain their tardiness or apparent unwillingness to respond.

Other options

Also don't forget that all your LinkedIn connections may have other contacts who are either not LinkedIn members by choice, or who are LinkedIn members but who haven't updated their networks. So it is always worth asking your LinkedIn connections directly to suggest any other avenues for you to follow, just in case.

Lastly, don't forget that if all else fails, you still have the fall-back option of trying to contact Chloe Carpenter directly via the phone, or sending a hard copy of your book proposal and a covering letter to her through the post.

Ideas for finding a publisher for your book via Facebook

Search the groups, pages and events for any contacts that are genuinely linked to the publishing industry; you never know what you might find. At the time of writing (July 2009), we found a great local low-cost workshop advertised on Facebook on how to get your book published, from an established author and expert in the publishing industry willing to share their insights and advice on everything from approaching publishers, the editing process, getting the right book jacket and demystifying advances and royalties.

When you have found a useful group, page or event, look through the list of members to see who you might be able to invite to join your network. Cross-check anyone you find in Facebook to LinkedIn (and vice versa). Having become a Facebook friend, they might also be willing to become a LinkedIn connection. You can check their Facebook profile for their email contact details and use this information to send an 'Introduction' email to them. Remember to personalise the LinkedIn text. But you need to avoid giving them the impression that you're stalking them so use your common sense here. As we have mentioned several times already, social networks thrive on reciprocity, so you need to be thinking in terms of 'what can I do for you?', as much as 'what do I need from you?'.

Publish extracts of your book in your Facebook Notes and point your friends to these updates. But be wary of the potential dangers of publishing your writing online. In May 2009, an English teacher in the UK, Leonora Rustamova, was sacked from her teaching job in a Yorkshire school for publishing a risqué novel online[205].

To build up your credibility and give potential publishers a flavour of what you can do, find some related interest groups on Facebook to join. Check the group's aims and objectives, and assuming it allows this activity, post questions and answers to the members and join the debate again to show case your knowledge and expertise in the field. For instance, if your book is about how to manage your money whilst being a student you could join:

- your college or university group (and any other Facebook groups for students),
- any groups run by the pastoral or student-support services at universities,
- groups related to banking and money management,
- other self-help groups.

You could even set up your own group and publish your top ten tips, write a tip of the week, or offer an Agony Aunt/Uncle column to your Facebook group.

How to deal with networking knock-backs

There's nothing ever good or bad, but thinking makes it so
Hamlet, Act II, Scene 2

It might be useful here to reflect on the skills of resilient people. We all know people who, after suffering a serious set-back such as a life-threatening illness or accident, redundancy or bankruptcy, manage to pick themselves up, dust themselves off and begin again with renewed vigour, interest and enthusiasm. Whilst they wouldn't wish their experience on their worst enemy, somehow they seem to have been made stronger and more determined by it. And we're

[205] http://news.bbc.co.uk/1/hi/england/west_yorkshire/8071857.stm

sure you also know others who give up their long-held goals and dreams at the slightest little hiccup. They may have hopes and ambitions of becoming a world-renowned sportsman, singer or scientist, but on coming up against a barrier such as not getting picked to represent their county, coming second in the local talent contest, or when their experiment fails to deliver the expected results, they pack it all in and decide they should stick to being a librarian or an accountant after all.

Sinking or swimming?

So how come some people have bags of resilience, and always seem to bounce back or come up smiling, and others don't? Are resilient people born that way, do they have thicker skins, better ideas, or more determination than others? What is it that enables them to try and try again, whereas other people see a set-back as a sign that they should give up and go back to what they were doing before?

In recent years, an increasing amount of psychology research[206] has been carried out to try to understand and answer these questions, and to provide guidance to those who get blown off course easily. After all, in today's ever-changing world, we need as much resilience as we can muster, particularly in business where life is becoming more and more competitive, complex and challenging. So what has this research uncovered that might help us build our robustness and powers of endurance so as to be less likely to succumb to set-backs, however challenging they are?

Well, you'll be delighted to know that, even though some people are naturally more resilient than others, the ability to adapt to and overcome challenges is something that we can all learn, given the will and the way. It boils down to being able to manage our negative emotions and thoughts so that they don't undermine our performance and persistence.

[206] For example, Masten, A. (2001). Ordinary magic: Resilience processes in development. *American Psychologist*, *56*(3), 227-238; Masten, A., & Reed, M. (2002). Resilience in development. *Handbook of positive psychology* (pp. 74-88). New York, NY US: Oxford University Press

We're taking for granted that you have the motivation to learn how to do this, so this next section will focus on the tips to help you tap into those optimistic beliefs, behaviours and skills that you already have which can be used to boost your coping ability, and enable you to bounce back swiftly and effectively.

Top tips for coming up smiling every time

1. Persist! But be realistic.

By all means, if your networking request for help is met with a 'no', you can always ask again, ask in a different way, or ask for some feedback, depending what the original request was. The number one skill in building your resilience is the ability to think flexibly. Of course you need a dose of dogged determination to succeed, but stubbornness and the inability to think differently is more likely to frustrate you than elate you.

You need to be able to reframe your request, or reframe your thoughts and beliefs in order to become truly resilient to set-backs.

2. Don't take a rejection personally

Although the majority of people you meet in life might be perfectly happy to help you move your career forward, and help you realise you dreams, the more people you meet the more likely you are to come across someone who can't, or won't, help you. This might be for all sorts of reasons which you can spend hours mulling over, but which you may never know.

It could simply be that they're too busy to help you. It could be that they don't know how. It could be that their cat died this morning and they have other things on their mind. It could be that they see you as a threat and don't want to help. Unless you know them very well, you can only surmise what the reason for their lack of support could be. But whatever it is, you have to adopt the mindset of 'win some, lose some'. It really is more about them than it is about you, so don't waste time trying to work out why, move on.

3. Don't blame your contacts

And whatever you do, don't bombard them with the same request over and over, or worse, send them a rude or curt email telling them you're disappointed that they can't (won't) assist. This will only weaken your relationship and could potentially scupper any hope of working with them in the future. If they say no they can't help you, respect their decision.

If, on the other hand, they don't reply to your email or phone call, by all means make a follow up call, but use some common sense and judgement here. There is a fine line between being an eager beaver and becoming a irritating thorn in their side.

4. Examine your emotions and beliefs objectively

Often our emotions and beliefs can get in the way of us performing effectively after we suffer a setback. Top resilience experts Drs Karen Reivich and Andrew Shatté[207] point out that it isn't the crisis we're experiencing that is the real problem, it's the way we think about it and respond to it that matters. Psychologists[208] recommend exploring emotions and beliefs objectively. World expert in Learned Optimism, Professor Martin Seligman advocates using several different techniques to challenge our thinking patterns, which in turn will change how we feel about the 'crisis' and lead to more useful (and emotionally acceptable) outcomes.

---

[207] Reivich, K. & Shatté, A. (2002). *The Resilience Factor*. New York. Broadway Books.
[208] Seligman, M.E.P (1990). *Learned optimism.* New York, Knopf.

Distract

Here are four very simple techniques you can learn to distract yourself when you know you are starting to worry about an issue, or your inner voice is starting to criticise you.

- Say 'STOP'!
- Write down the thoughts that are bothering you.
- Schedule some time later in your day to think about the issue.
- Focus intently on another object, such as a piece of jewellery or the pencil in your hand.

Dispute

Write down the thoughts that are concerning you and objectively unpack them one by one. What is the evidence for this? Is there another alternative explanation? Explore the consequences – if there is some truth in what you are thinking, then put it in perspective. Finally, ask yourself how useful it is to think like that; if it isn't, use one of the distraction techniques above.

Distance

Initially you may find it difficult to dispute your own thoughts; it takes practise. So try to insert some objectivity into the exercise by imagining that someone else is saying these things – usually they sound less believable then. Take every opportunity you can find to argue with yourself!

Having looked at your beliefs from every which way, you then need to reframe them into something more realistic, and more helpful.

One very effective exercise, recommended by Positive Psychologist Barbara Fredrickson, the researcher behind the broaden-and-build theory of positive emotions, is to create your own 'Resilience Bank'.

You can do this by collecting examples of photos, emails, letters or indeed any mementos which raise your spirits or inspire you when you look at them. Perhaps you have a photo of you on graduation day, a photo of your team celebrating the end of a challenging project, an email from your favourite lecturer or teacher, a letter of recommendation from a client, a Thank-You card from someone you helped out in the past, an email acknowledging your hard work from a boss or some inspiring quotations you found in a book or online. Think of as many things as possible which increase your motivation when you look at them and collect them together in one place: this can be a simple folder, wallet or journal, or even your mobile phone or PDA. Then whenever you need a psychological pick-me-up, just take a look at your Resilience Bank and you'll feel back on track in no time.

Conclusion

We wrote this book with two main aims in mind: firstly to help those of you who are already established managers, and who are part of the X Generation or older, that is, people who can remember life as it was before the internet, mobile phones and PDAs, and who may feel uncomfortable about using social networking for anything other than posting a few family snaps or keeping an eye on what their teenage kids are up to. We hope we have persuaded you that social networking is also an important business tool; it provides you with the chance to further your professional goals in ways you may not have previously considered. Secondly, we wanted to help those of you from the Y Generation or younger, people who have grown up with the internet and who are happy to be 'connected' 24/7. For you, using various social networking sites to communicate is second nature, and you need no help with the technicalities. But although you're very confident with social networking as a tool for connecting to friends, you may be less assured when it comes to networking to advance your career or find your dream job. You may also be less aware of the serious implications for your later working life of making your personal details public property.

So we hope this book has given you some food for thought. Social networking is rapidly changing how we interact, and provides an enormous opportunity to connect , work together and do business in ways that we would never have imagined possible twenty years ago. Facebook, LinkedIn and Twitter are not just about passing the time of day with friends (although that's important too). They allow us to forge new relationships, maintain hundreds of connections and present ourselves and what we do in unique ways. Whether you love it or hate it, online social networking is here to stay; you cannot turn back the digital tide.

Are you ready to take control?

Glossary

360° Endorsements: endorsements of your performance or achievements made by your boss, peer group and the people who work for you.

Blogroll: a list of the blogs and websites you recommend, maintained in a specific section on your blog (or website). Blogrolling works on the reciprocity principle (a bit like following on Twitter)

Cached: a temporary storage area on the net where previously accessed data is stored for rapid access. Once the data is stored in the cache, future use can be made by accessing the cached copy rather than re-fetching the original data. However changes to the original source do not change the copy, so the copy can be out of date.

Instant Messaging (IM): real-time text-based communication between two or more people. The text is conveyed by devices over a network, such as the internet.

MS-DOS: Microsoft Disk Operating System, replaced by Windows.

Multi-Level Marketing: 'pyramid' marketing where promoters are rewarded not just on the products/services they themselves promote, but on those promoted by people they introduce.

Netizens: internet users

Y Generation (also called **Net Generation** or **Millenials**): an individual born after 1980

Appendix
Using Email

Top Tips for writing email:

N Never use CAPITAL LETTERS or excessive punctuation!!???@***!!!!

E Empathise – how will the recipient feel reading your email? Consider the tone and style of what you write – don't forget that you are dealing with another human being.

T Take care with your terminology, especially acronyms.

I Include bullet points to make your message concise and clear.

Q Quality counts: just because email is informal, doesn't mean you shouldn't use the spellchecker.

U Use plain English: short words and phrases are better than long or complex ones. The Plain English Campaign website[209] is an excellent source of free materials.

E Ensure you include an appropriate greeting or acknowledgement including the recipient's name, and sign-off in your emails.

T Think about the sensitivity of your message – might it be more appropriate to phone the person instead?

T Think twice before you hit the 'send' button – are you sending your email to the right person for the right reasons?

E Ensure you use the subject line appropriately – if necessary, fill it in last (but don't forget!)

[209] http://www.plainenglish.co.uk/free_guides.html

Netiquette for Mailing Lists (Listservs)[210]

- Do not blame the system administrator for the behaviour of the system users.
- Consider that a large audience will see your posts. That may include your present or your next boss. Take care in what you write. Remember too, that mailing lists and Newsgroups are frequently archived, and that your words may be stored for a very long time in a place to which many people have access.
- Assume that individuals speak for themselves, and what they say does not represent their organization (unless stated explicitly).
- Messages and articles should be brief and to the point. Don't wander off-topic, don't ramble and don't send mail or post messages solely to point out other people's errors in typing or spelling. These, more than any other behaviour, mark you as an immature beginner.
- Subject lines should follow the conventions of the group.
- Advertising is welcomed on some lists and Newsgroups, and abhorred on others! This is another example of knowing your audience before you post. Unsolicited advertising which is completely off-topic will most certainly guarantee that you get a lot of hate mail.
- Be careful when you reply to messages or postings. Frequently replies are sent back to the address which originated the post. You may accidentally send a personal response to a great many people, embarrassing all involved. It's best to type in the address instead of relying on 'reply.'
- If you find a personal message has gone to a list or group, send an apology to the person and to the group.
- If you should find yourself in a disagreement with one person, make your responses to each other via email rather than

[210] For the full list of IETF Netiquette rules, see http://www.faqs.org/ftp/rfc/pdf/rfc1855.txt.pdf

continue to send messages to the list or the group. If you are debating a point on which the group might have some interest, you may summarize for them later.

- Don't get involved in flame wars. Neither post nor respond to incendiary material.
- Avoid sending messages or posting articles which are no more than gratuitous replies to replies.
- Send subscribe and unsubscribe messages to the appropriate address. Although some mailing list software is smart enough to catch these, not all can ferret these out. It is your responsibility to learn how the lists work, and to send the correct mail to the correct place. Be sure you know the conventions used by the lists to which you subscribe.
- Save the subscription messages for any lists you join. These usually tell you how to unsubscribe as well.
- In general, it's not possible to retrieve messages once you have sent them. Even your system administrator will not be able to get a message back once you have sent it. This means you must make sure you really want the message to go as you have written it.
- Consider unsubscribing when you cannot check your mail for an extended period. To this we would add one further point: if you enable the 'Out of Office' message on your email system instead, make sure you exclude the Listserv.
- Some mailing lists are private. Do not send mail to these lists uninvited. Do not report mail from these lists to a wider audience.

Index